STRATEGY AND MISSION OF THE DHS SCIENCE AND TECHNOLOGY DIRECTORATE

JOINT HEARING

BEFORE THE

SUBCOMMITTEE ON CYBERSECURITY,
INFRASTRUCTURE PROTECTION,
AND SECURITY TECHNOLOGIES

OF THE

COMMITTEE ON HOMELAND SECURITY
HOUSE OF REPRESENTATIVES

Serial No. 113–83

AND THE

SUBCOMMITTEE ON RESEARCH AND TECHNOLOGY

OF THE

COMMITTEE ON SCIENCE, SPACE,
AND TECHNOLOGY
HOUSE OF REPRESENTATIVES

Serial No. 113–91

ONE HUNDRED THIRTEENTH CONGRESS

SECOND SESSION

SEPTEMBER 9, 2014

Printed for the use of the Committee on Homeland Security and the
Committee on Science, Space, and Technology

Available via the World Wide Web: http://www.gpo.gov/fdsys/

U.S. GOVERNMENT PUBLISHING OFFICE

92–900 PDF   WASHINGTON : 2015

For sale by the Superintendent of Documents, U.S. Government Publishing Office
Internet: bookstore.gpo.gov   Phone: toll free (866) 512–1800; DC area (202) 512–1800
Fax: (202) 512–2104   Mail: Stop IDCC, Washington, DC 20402–0001

COMMITTEE ON HOMELAND SECURITY

MICHAEL T. MCCAUL, Texas, *Chairman*

LAMAR SMITH, Texas
PETER T. KING, New York
MIKE ROGERS, Alabama
PAUL C. BROUN, Georgia
CANDICE S. MILLER, Michigan, *Vice Chair*
PATRICK MEEHAN, Pennsylvania
JEFF DUNCAN, South Carolina
TOM MARINO, Pennsylvania
JASON CHAFFETZ, Utah
STEVEN M. PALAZZO, Mississippi
LOU BARLETTA, Pennsylvania
RICHARD HUDSON, North Carolina
STEVE DAINES, Montana
SUSAN W. BROOKS, Indiana
SCOTT PERRY, Pennsylvania
MARK SANFORD, South Carolina
CURTIS CLAWSON, Florida

BENNIE G. THOMPSON, Mississippi
LORETTA SANCHEZ, California
SHEILA JACKSON LEE, Texas
YVETTE D. CLARKE, New York
BRIAN HIGGINS, New York
CEDRIC L. RICHMOND, Louisiana
WILLIAM R. KEATING, Massachusetts
RON BARBER, Arizona
DONDALD M. PAYNE, JR., New Jersey
BETO O'ROURKE, Texas
FILEMON VELA, Texas
ERIC SWALWELL, California
VACANCY
VACANCY

BRENDAN P. SHIELDS, *Staff Director*
JOAN O'HARA, *Acting Chief Counsel*
MICHAEL S. TWINCHEK, *Chief Clerk*
I. LANIER AVANT, *Minority Staff Director*

———

SUBCOMMITTEE ON CYBERSECURITY, INFRASTRUCTURE PROTECTION, AND SECURITY TECHNOLOGIES

PATRICK MEEHAN, Pennsylvania, *Chairman*

MIKE ROGERS, Alabama
TOM MARINO, Pennsylvania
JASON CHAFFETZ, Utah
STEVE DAINES, Montana
SCOTT PERRY, Pennsylvania, *Vice Chair*
MICHAEL T. MCCAUL, Texas *(ex officio)*

YVETTE D. CLARKE, New York
WILLIAM R. KEATING, Massachusetts
FILEMON VELA, Texas
VACANCY
BENNIE G. THOMPSON, Mississippi *(ex officio)*

ALEX MANNING, *Subcommittee Staff Director*
DENNIS TERRY, *Subcommittee Clerk*

COMMITTEE ON SCIENCE, SPACE, AND TECHNOLOGY

LAMAR S. SMITH, Texas, *Chairman*

DANA ROHRABACHER, California
RALPH M. HALL, Texas
F. JAMES SENSENBRENNER, JR., Wisconsin
FRANK D. LUCAS, Oklahoma
RANDY NEUGEBAUER, Texas
MICHAEL T. McCAUL, Texas
PAUL C. BROUN, Georgia
STEVEN M. PALAZZO, Mississippi
MO BROOKS, Alabama
RANDY HULTGREN, Illinois
LARRY BUCSHON, Indiana
STEVE STOCKMAN, Texas
BILL POSEY, Florida
CYNTHIA LUMMIS, Wyoming
DAVID SCHWEIKERT, Arizona
THOMAS MASSIE, Kentucky
KEVIN CRAMER, North Dakota
JIM BRIDENSTINE, Oklahoma
RANDY WEBER, Texas
CHRIS COLLINS, New York
BILL JOHNSON, Ohio

EDDIE BERNICE JOHNSON, Texas
ZOE LOFGREN, California
DANIEL LIPINSKI, Illinois
DONNA F. EDWARDS, Maryland
FREDERICA S. WILSON, Florida
SUZANNE BONAMICI, Oregon
ERIC SWALWELL, California
DAN MAFFEI, New York
ALAN GRAYSON, Florida
JOSEPH KENNEDY III, Massachusetts
SCOTT PETERS, California
DEREK KILMER, Washington
AMI BERA, California
ELIZABETH ESTY, Connecticut
MARC VEASEY, Texas
JULIA BROWNLEY, California
ROBIN KELLY, Illinois
KATHERINE CLARK, Massachusetts

———

SUBCOMMITTEE ON RESEARCH AND TECHNOLOGY

LARRY BUCSHON, Indiana, *Chairman*

STEVEN M. PALAZZO, Mississippi
MO BROOKS, Alabama
RANDY HULTGREN, Illinois
STEVE STOCKMAN, Texas
CYNTHIA LUMMIS, Wyoming
DAVID SCHWEIKERT, Arizona
THOMAS MASSIE, Kentucky
JIM BRIDENSTINE, Oklahoma
CHRIS COLLINS, New York
BILL JOHNSON, Ohio
LAMAR S. SMITH, Texas

DANIEL LIPINSKI, Illinois
FEDERICA WILSON, Florida
ZOE LOFGREN, California
SCOTT PETERS, California
AMI BERA, California
DEREK KILMER, Washington
ELIZABETH ESTY, Connecticut
ROBIN KELLY, Illinois
EDDIE BERNICE JOHNSON, Texas

CONTENTS

———

STRATEGY AND MISSION OF THE DHS SCIENCE AND TECHNOLOGY DIRECTORATE

Tuesday, September 9, 2014

U.S. HOUSE OF REPRESENTATIVES,
COMMITTEE ON HOMELAND SECURITY,
SUBCOMMITTEE ON CYBERSECURITY,
INFRASTRUCTURE PROTECTION, AND
SECURITY TECHNOLOGIES, AND
U.S. HOUSE OF REPRESENTATIVES,
COMMITTEE ON SCIENCE, SPACE, AND TECHNOLOGY,
SUBCOMMITTEE ON RESEARCH AND TECHNOLOGY,
Washington, DC.

The subcommittees met, pursuant to call, at 10:05 a.m., in Room 311, Cannon House Office Building, Hon. Patrick Meehan [Chairman of the Subcommittee on Cybersecurity, Infrastructure Protection, and Security Technologies] presiding.

Present from Subcommittee on Cybersecurity, Infrastructure Protection, and Security Technologies: Representatives Meehan, Rogers, Perry, and Thompson.

Present from Subcommittee on Research and Technology: Representatives Buschon, Hultgren, Collins, Johnson, Lipinski, Peters, Esty, and Kelly.

Also present: Representatives Payne and Smith.

Mr. MEEHAN. The Subcommittee on Cybersecurity, Infrastructure Protection, and Security Technologies of the Committee of Homeland Security and the Subcommittee on Research and Technology of the Committee on Science, Space, and Technology will come to order.

The subcommittees are jointly meeting today to examine the strategy and mission of the Science and Technology Directorate at the Department of Homeland Security. Good morning, and thank you for being here this morning.

I now recognize myself for an opening statement. I would like to thank everyone for attending this important joint hearing on the strategy and mission of the DHS Science and Technology Directorate. I would particularly like to thank Ranking Member Payne as well as Chairman Bucshon and Ranking Member Lipinski of the Science, Space, and Technology's Research and Technology Subcommittee for their joint participation. I often think that we do so much better work when we can work together on these. Since both committees share jurisdiction, it is helpful we are holding this oversight hearing while we collaborate on writing an authorization bill.

I would also like that thank our witnesses: Dr. Reginald "Reggie" Brothers, the new under secretary for S&T; and David Maurer from the GAO. I look forward to hearing from both of you on the challenges facing the directorate and how we can help ensure S&T is able to fulfill its mission.

The DHS Science and Technology Directorate was established by Congress to be the primary research and development arm of the Department of Homeland Security. In this role, S&T manages science and technology research and provides acquisition support for the Department's operational components. It works with partners to do basic research and provide technology solutions to first responders.

It is no secret that the Science and Technology Directorate has had its challenges since its creation. But despite several restructuring and close Congressional oversight, the S&T Directorate continues to face difficulties in fulfilling its mission. Problems with priority setting and strategic planning for the directorate's R&D programs, as well as balancing incremental efforts with high-risk, high-reward research remain a challenge. In addition, there continues to be challenges with working with the operational components in both research and acquisition support activities.

Our committees have been working together to develop authorizing language for the S&T Directorate to give it the clarity, structure, and tools it needs, while ensuring it remains accountable. I look forward to working with everyone here as we develop this legislation.

We appreciate that Dr. Brothers, who was just confirmed—and congratulations on that—to his post as under secretary in April. We don't expect all these problems to be solved overnight. But that said, we are interested in hearing your ideas on how to get, and to keep, the S&T Directorate on track.

Dr. Brothers recently briefed our staff and will discuss, in his testimony, the establishment of four key visionary goals in which the S&T will focus their efforts. While goals are important, we are also interested in hearing the strategy and implementation plan to make those goals a reality, including time lines and metrics to the extent you feel that they can be—those measurements can be attached to those goals. S&T has a unique position and opportunity to be, as you said in your written testimony, the glue between operational elements. I look forward to hearing about specific successes that S&T has accomplished working with operational components.

Just as important, we look forward to hearing how S&T intends to balance the long-term research agenda with the short-term operational technology development and acquisition support.

Again, I would like to thank the witnesses, as well as our Science Committee colleagues, for participating in the hearing today.

[The statement of Chairman Meehan follows:]

STATEMENT OF CHAIRMAN PATRICK MEEHAN

SEPTEMBER 9, 2014

I would like to thank everyone for attending this important joint hearing on the strategy and mission of the DHS Science and Technology (S&T) Directorate. I would particularly like to thank Ranking Member Clarke as well as Chairman Bucshon and Ranking Member Lipinski of the Science and Technology Research Subcommittee for their participation. Since both committees share jurisdiction it is helpful that we are holding this oversight hearing together while we collaborate on writing an authorization bill. I would also like to thank our witnesses, Dr. Reginald

"Reggie" Brothers, the new under secretary for S&T and David Maurer from GAO and I look forward to hearing from both of you on the challenges facing the directorate and how we can help ensure S&T is able to fulfill its mission.

The DHS Science and Technology Directorate was established by Congress to be the primary research and development arm of the Department of Homeland Security. In this role, S&T manages science and technology research and provides acquisition support for the Department's operational components, and works with partners to do basic research and provide technology solutions to first responders.

It is no secret that the Science and Technology Directorate has had challenges since its creation. Despite several restructurings and close Congressional oversight, the S&T Directorate continues to face difficulties in fulfilling its mission. Problems with priority setting and strategic planning for the directorate's R&D programs as well as balancing incremental efforts with high-risk, high-reward research remain a challenge. In addition, there continue to be challenges with working with the operational components in both research and acquisition support activities.

Our committees have been working together to develop authorizing language for the S&T Directorate to give it the clarity, structure, and tools it needs while ensuring it remains accountable. I look forward to working with everyone here as we develop that legislation.

We appreciate that Dr. Brothers was just confirmed to his post as Under Secretary in April and we don't expect all of these problems to be solved overnight. That said, we are interested in hearing his ideas on how to get and keep the S&T Directorate on track. Dr. Brothers recently briefed our staff, and will discuss in his testimony, the establishment of four key visionary goals on which S&T will focus their efforts. And while goals are important, we are also interested in hearing the strategy and implementation plan to make those goals a reality including time lines and metrics as well.

S&T has a unique position and opportunity to be, as you said in your written testimony, "the glue between operational elements." We look forward hearing about specific successes that S&T has accomplished working with operational components. And just as important, we look forward to hearing how S&T intends to balance the long-term research agenda with short-term operational technology development and acquisition support.

Again, I would like to thank the witnesses as well as our Science, Space, and Technology Committee colleagues for participating in this hearing today. With that, I yield the balance of my time.

Mr. MEEHAN. With that, I yield back the balance of my time, and I now recognize the Ranking Minority Member, the gentleman who is representing the subcommittee today, from New Jersey, Mr. Payne, for any opening comments he may have.

Mr. PAYNE. Thank you, Chairman Meehan, and to Chairman Bucshon, to my Ranking Member, Mr. Thompson. I have a statement from the subcommittee Ranking Member, Yvette D. Clarke, who apologizes for not being able to be here today. I'll read that now.

Thank you, Chairman Meehan and Chairman Bucshon for convening this joint hearing of the Science and Technology Directorate. I want to especially welcome Ranking Member Lipinski and our colleagues from the Subcommittee on Research and Technology.

Dr. Brothers, it is good to have you back before this subcommittee. Mr. Maurer, thank you for agreeing to give us your perspective, and we are pleased to have you here today. S&T is an essential component of the Department's efforts. I know many of us are eager to hear about the new vision and priorities at the directorate. The mission of the S&T Directorate is to strengthen America's security and resiliency by providing innovative science and technology solutions for the homeland security enterprise.

In order to meet the needs of this diverse stakeholder, who covers all of DHS missions in areas, S&T strives to rapidly develop and deliver knowledge, analysis, and innovative solutions that advance the mission of the Department. S&T also leverages technical expertise to assist the efforts of the DHS components to establish operational requirements and to select and acquire needed technologies. The ultimate goal of S&T, as I see it, is to strengthen the Homeland Security's first responders' capabilities to protect the homeland and respond to disaster.

Along the way, S&T must help foster a culture of innovation and learning across DHS that speaks to the challenges with scientist and technical rigor. In 2009, spurred by the findings of several reports about S&T—especially one performed by the National Academy of Public Administration—this subcommittee initiated its own year-long comprehensive review of the directorate. Our purpose was to identify areas within the directorate that could use a fresh set of eyes and additional oversight, or modifications, to legislative authorities. As a result, we produced a comprehensive bipartisan bill which passed the House unanimously in 2010.

In doing so, we reviewed the Homeland Security Act and the Department's use of the authorities that Congress had vested in it, and I am hoping that some of these things we learned during that process can be used in future authorization efforts. One of the things we did learn was that such a large and complex portfolio and—the directorate has, it is difficult to craft a cohesive strategy. Our analysis suggested that the Department had not developed a clear risk-based methodology to determine what research projects to fund, how much to fund, and how to evaluate a project's effectiveness or usefulness. These questions remain today.

In my opinion, the directorate will never achieve success unless research rules and metrics are more fully established. I am anxious to hear of any plans that the under secretary may have in mind to keep the directorate moving forward during these challenging times. Striving to do more with less is always the hallmark of an efficiently-run effort of any type. But trying to protect our citizens and the Nation, with programs that are backed by unfunded and depleted science and technology research assets is another matter.

Thank you, Mr. Chairman, and I yield back.

[The statement of Ranking Member Clarke follows:]

STATEMENT OF RANKING MEMBER YVETTE D. CLARKE

SEPTEMBER 9, 2014

Thank you Chairman Meehan and Chairman Bucshon for convening this joint hearing on the Science and Technology Directorate, and I want to especially welcome Ranking Member Lipinski and our colleagues from the Subcommittee on Research and Technology. Dr. Brothers, it is good to see you back before this subcommittee, and Mr. Maurer, thank you for agreeing to give us your perspective, and we are pleased to have you here today.

S&T is an essential component of the Department's efforts, and I know many of us are eager to hear about a new vision and priorities at the directorate. The mission of the S&T Directorate is to strengthen America's security and resiliency by providing innovative science and technology solutions for the Homeland Security Enterprise.

In order to meet the needs of its diverse stakeholders who cover all DHS mission areas, S&T strives to rapidly develop and deliver knowledge, analyses, and innovative solutions that advance the mission of the Department.

S&T also leverages technical expertise to assist the efforts of the DHS components to establish operational requirements and to select and acquire needed technologies. The ultimate goal of S&T, as I see it, is to strengthen the Homeland Security First Responders' capabilities to protect the homeland and respond to disaster.

Along the way, S&T must help foster a culture of innovation and learning across DHS that speaks to challenges with scientific and technical rigor. In 2009, spurred by the findings of several reports about S&T, especially one performed by the National Academy of Public Administration, this subcommittee initiated its own year-long comprehensive review of the directorate.

Our purpose was to identify areas within the directorate that could use a fresh set of eyes and additional oversight or modifications to legislative authorities. As a result, we produced a comprehensive, bipartisan bill, which passed the House unanimously in 2010.

In doing so, we reviewed the Homeland Security Act and the Department's use of the authorities the Congress has vested in it. I am hoping that some of the things we learned during that process can be used in future authorization efforts.

One of the things we did learn was that with such a large and complex portfolio, the directorate has found it difficult to craft a cohesive strategy. Our analysis suggested that the Department had not developed a clear risk-based methodology to determine what research projects to fund, how much to fund, and how to evaluate a project's effectiveness or usefulness. These questions remain today.

In my opinion, the directorate will never achieve success unless research rules and metrics are more fully established, and I am anxious to hear of any plans that the Under Secretary may have in mind to keep the directorate moving forward during these challenging times.

Striving to do more with less is always the hallmark of an efficiently-run effort—of any type—but trying to protect our citizens and Nation with programs that are backed by underfunded and depleted science and technology research assets, is another matter.

Mr. MEEHAN. I want to thank the gentleman from New Jersey.

Now I would like to recognize my co-chair for the hearing today, the gentleman from Illinois, or from Indiana, Mr. Bucshon, for any statement that he may have.

Mr. BUCSHON. Thank you, Chairman Meehan. I am happy to welcome everyone to this joint hearing on the Department of Homeland Security Science and Technology Directorate. As we work on the potential reauthorization of the S&T Directorate, this hearing will provide us with background information needed from the under secretary for science and technology, who recently took on his post at the Department, and from the Government Accountability Office that has produced a number of reports focused on the directorate.

In July, the Research and Technology Subcommittee, which I chair, held a hearing looking at the S&T Directorate's work related to border security technology. That hearing, as well as today's, should offer valuable details to inform our work on our subcommittees. Established in 2002 in the Homeland Security Act, the Directorate for Science and Technology has primary responsibility for bringing new technologies to full readiness at DHS. The mission of an S&T directorate is to, "to strengthen America's security and resilience by providing knowledge, products, and innovative technology solutions for the homeland security enterprise."

My district in southwest Indiana is home to Naval Surface Warfare Center Crane, whose personnel and facilities provide the Department of Defense with state-of-the-art technology. Given this, I am particularly interested in learning how existing technologies perhaps used for the Department of Defense purposes are being, and can be, utilized in different ways for securing the homeland. Twelve years ago, the Homeland Security Act tasked the S&T Directorate with the coordination and integration of research, development, demonstration, and testing and evaluation activities at DHS.

Unfortunately, the S&T Directorate has not yet been able to accomplish this task. I look forward to hearing from both of our witnesses about how the directorate can move forward to carry out this important role. Today's hearing should provide us with invaluable insights and oversight of the S&T Directorate. I look forward to hearing from both of our witnesses.

Thank you, Chairman Meehan, and I yield back.

[The statement of Chairman Bucshon follows:]

STATEMENT OF CHAIRMAN LARRY BUSCHON

SEPTEMBER 9, 2014

Thank you Chairman Meehan. I am happy to welcome everyone to this joint hearing on the Department of Homeland Security's Science and Technology Directorate (S&T Directorate).

As we work on the potential reauthorization of the S&T Directorate, this hearing will provide us with background and information needed from the Under Secretary for Science and Technology who recently took on his post at the Department, and the Government Accountability Office that has produced a number of reports focused on the Directorate.

In July, the Research and Technology Subcommittee held a hearing looking at the S&T Directorate's work related to border security technology. That hearing, as well as today's, should offer valuable details to inform our work.

Established in 2002 in the Homeland Security Act, the Directorate for Science and Technology has primary responsibility for bringing new technologies to full readiness at DHS.

The mission of the S&T Directorate is "to strengthen America's security and resiliency by providing knowledge products and innovative technology solutions for the Homeland Security Enterprise." My district in southwest Indiana is home to Naval Surface Warfare Center Crane, whose personnel and facilities provide the Department of Defense with state-of-the-art technology.

Given this, I am particularly interested in learning how existing technologies, perhaps used for Department of Defense purposes, are being and can be utilized in different ways for securing the Homeland.

Twelve years ago, the Homeland Security Act tasked the S&T Directorate with the coordination and integration of the research, development, demonstration, and testing and evaluation activities of DHS. Unfortunately, the S&T Directorate has not yet been able to accomplish this task. I look forward to hearing from both of our witnesses about how the directorate can move forward to carry out this important role.

Today's hearing should provide us with invaluable insights and oversight of the S&T directorate. I look forward to hearing from both of our witnesses. Thank you Chairman Meehan and I yield back.

Mr. MEEHAN. I want to thank the gentleman. I will now recognize the gentleman from Illinois. But I recognize, as well, that when you mix up Indiana and Illinois during Big 10 football season you do so at great peril.

But Mr. Lipinski, for any comments he may have.

Mr. LIPINSKI. Thank you, Mr. Chairman. I went to Northwestern so Illinois isn't my team. But before I start, I wanted to ask unanimous consent to insert in the record an opening statement from Ranking Member Eddie Bernice Johnson of the Committee on Science, Space, and Technology.

Mr. MEEHAN. Without objection, so ordered.

[The statement of Ranking Member Johnson follows:]

STATEMENT OF RANKING MEMBER EDDIE BERNICE JOHNSON

SEPTEMBER 9, 2014

Thank you Mr. Chairman. As the Ranking Member of the Science, Space, and Technology Committee, I am pleased to see this collaborative effort by these two committees as we hear from the Under Secretary for Science and Technology at DHS and GAO. Thank you to the witnesses for being here. I hope this cross-committee bipartisan collaboration continues as we work to reauthorize the S&T Directorate.

The Department's research activities aim to deliver the latest technologies and innovative solutions to the agents in the field. These technologies act as a force multiplier to protect our borders, our cities, and our communities. The homeland security threat landscape is constantly changing and innovative research allows us to stay ahead of those who wish to do us harm. This complex challenge requires the greatest minds and most talented workforce. Dr. Brothers, I look forward to hearing how you are tapping into and improving the DHS workforce to ensure the best leaders and decision makers are at the table to push the Department's research operations to new levels.

In addition to a strong workforce, DHS has five National laboratories and access to the excellent facilities and strong technical support at Department of Energy labs. DHS also has 12 university-based Centers of Excellence, an advanced research projects agency, and a growing industrial base. The tools are all there. Where S&T has fallen short is in carrying out the basics of good Government: Strategic planning, coordination across the agency, and adequate testing and evaluation. These problems must be fixed.

I look forward to hearing from you, Dr. Brothers, on the changes you will be putting in place to ensure DHS R&D investments are well-managed.

Again, thank you Mr. Chairman for holding this hearing and I yield back the balance of my time.

Mr. LIPINSKI. Thank you. I want to thank Chairman Meehan and Chairman Bucshon for calling this hearing today. I welcome the opportunity to join with my colleagues on the Homeland Security Committee to discuss the important work being done at the Department of Homeland Security's Science and Technology Directorate. I also want to thank our witnesses for being here. Under Secretary Brothers, I look forward to hearing about your plans and progress so far for the S&T Directorate. Mr. Maurer, it is good to see you again. We had a good hearing back in the Science, Space, and Technology Committee in July.

It is no secret that the creation of DHS as a single agency constructed from several existing agencies with diverse missions generated a number of management challenges. The S&T Directorate's task of providing high-quality scientific and technical support for all of the agency's missions is undoubtedly a daunting one. Having said that, I am disappointed that the success of the S&T Directorate continues to be limited by a lack of effective strategy and a lack of coordination resulting in some costly and, likely, preventable failures. This must change.

Under Secretary Brothers, I am interested to hear from you about the policy management changes you are putting in place to shift the S&T Directorate toward a more focused and strategic operation. I want to make sure everyone understands that, you know, you are new to this—relatively new to this position. As I said to you before we began, this is a very daunting task that you have. But we are all happy to work with you to help you succeed in that. As you put together a strategic plan for S&T, I hope you will look critically at customer needs, your relationship with the operational components, the balance between short- and long-term research, and lessons learned from past failures.

Visionary goals and detailed objectives can be helpful, but those need to be coupled with effective policies and practices to ensure success. The end-users of S&T Directorate research are varied and have a wide range of technical and operational needs. The end-users span from first responders and private industry to Border Patrol Agents and TSA screeners. I would like to hear how the directorate seeks to prioritize these end-users and fit their needs into the broader R&D strategy, as indicated by DHS risk analyses.

Successful technology development also requires researchers and end-users to be communicating and collaborating at each stage of the R&D process. I think it is fair to say that the relationship between S&T and the operational components has not always been productive. I look forward to hearing what S&T is doing to improve these relationships and how they define their role within each phase of the technology development process. In addition, operational mission needs often demand tangible outcomes and deliverables.

However, I am very concerned that DHS is not striking the right balance between critical basic research and applied technology development. Without long-term investment in the Department, the Nation will not have the scientific foundation for new homeland security technologies in the future.

Finally, as Science Committee Members heard at our July hearing, social science has played an important role in the technology development, testing, and evaluation processes. We have seen how the most advanced technologies can end as failures because the developers do not consider how the operators in the field will use the technology.

I am interesting to hear what methods are in place now to ensure that human factors are considered during technology development and acquisition. Once again, Dr. Brothers, you have quite a task before you. I look forward to working with you and, hopefully, providing you with some of the tools you need to improve the R&D efforts at DHS. Most importantly keep the American homeland safe.

Thank you, Mr. Chairman, and I yield back the balance of my time.

[The statement of Ranking Member Lipinski follows:]

STATEMENT OF RANKING MEMBER DANIEL LIPINSKI

SEPTEMBER 9, 2014

Thank you to Chairman Meehan and Chairman Bucshon for calling this hearing today. I welcome the opportunity to join with my colleagues on the Homeland Security Committee to discuss the important work being done at the Department of Homeland Security's Science and Technology Directorate.

I also want to thank our witnesses for being here. Under Secretary Brothers, I look forward to hearing about your plans and progress so far with the S&T Directorate. Mr. Maurer, it is good to see you again.

It is no secret that the creation of DHS as a single agency constructed from several existing agencies with diverse missions generated a number of management challenges. The S&T Directorate's task of providing high-quality scientific and technical support for all of the agency's missions is undoubtedly a daunting one. Having said that, I am disappointed that the success of the S&T Directorate continues to be limited by the lack of an effective strategy and a lack of coordination, resulting in some costly and likely preventable failures. This must change.

Under Secretary Brothers, I am interested to hear from you about the policy and management changes you are putting in place to shift the S&T Directorate toward a more focused and strategic operation. As you put together a strategic plan for S&T, I hope you will look critically at customer needs, your relationship with the operational components, the balance between short- and long-term research, and lessons learned from past failures. Visionary goals and detailed objectives can be helpful, but those need to be coupled with effective policies and practices to ensure success.

The end-users of S&T Directorate research are varied and have a wide range of technical and operational needs. The end-users span from first responders and private industry to Border Patrol Agents and TSA Screeners. I would like to hear how the Directorate seeks to prioritize these end-users and fit their needs into the broader R&D strategy as indicated by DHS risk analyses.

Successful technology development also requires researchers and end-users to be communicating and collaborating at each stage of the R&D process. I think it is fair to say that the relationship between S&T and the operational components has not always been productive. I look forward to hearing what S&T is doing to improve these relationships and how they define their role within each phase of the technology development process.

In addition, operational mission needs often demand tangible outcomes and deliverables. However, I am very concerned that DHS is not striking the right balance between critical basic research and applied technology development. Without long-term investments, the Department and the Nation will not have the scientific foundation for new homeland security technologies in the future.

Finally, as Science Committee Members heard at our July hearing, social sciences play an important role in the technology development, testing, and evaluation processes. We have seen how the most advanced technologies can end as failures because the developers do not consider how the operators in the field will use the technology. I am interested to hear what methods are in place now to ensure that human factors are considered during technology development and acquisition.

Once again, Dr. Brothers, you have quite the task before you. I look forward to working with you and hopefully providing you with some of the tools you need to improve the R&D efforts at DHS, and most importantly keep the American homeland safe.

Thank you Mr. Chairman, I yield back the balance of my time.

Mr. MEEHAN. Yes, I thank the gentleman. I know the Chairman of the Science, Space, and Technology Committee expects to be here and to make an opening statement, which I will recognize him when he arrives. But we are also very grateful to have at the hearing today the Ranking Member of the full Committee on Homeland Security, the gentleman from Mississippi.

I invite the gentleman if he would like to make any comments before we begin.

Mr. THOMPSON. Thank you, Mr. Chairman. Promise you I will be brief.

As I said, thank you and thank Chairman Bucshon for convening this joint hearing on the Science and Technology Directorate. I want to especially welcome Ranking Member Lipinski and our colleagues from the Subcommittee on Research and Technology. I join you in welcoming both Under Secretary Brothers to the committee, and Mr. Maurer on the Government Accountability Office, and look forward to today's testimony.

Research and development on technologies is a key component of DHS's efforts to detect, prevent, and mitigate terrorist threats. Given the size of DHS, its role in the Federal Government, and the dynamics of the current threat picture R&D should be a priority. DHS should have a cohesive policy that defines responsibility for coordinating R&D and mechanisms to attract all DHS R&D projects. Unfortunately, this is not the case. Multiple entities across DHS conduct various types of R&D in pursuit of their respective missions.

According to GAO, DHS does not have a Department-wide policy defining R&D, or guidance directing components how to report R&D activities and investments. Consequently, it leaves Congress to question where the Science and Technology Directorate fits in this picture. Does S&T have the ability to maintain oversight of its investment in R&D across the Department? Where are S&T's limitations on its ability to oversee components of R&D efforts and align them with agency-wide goals and priorities? This fragmented approach, to allow R&D within S&T to be an easy target for all sets.

As my colleagues across the aisle continue to support extreme budget cuts that affect the funding levels for the Department, programs that are not clear in their mission do not have metrics to illustrate their value heighten their vulnerability. Congress recognizes that threat picture is evolving. Accordingly, it should make sense to continue to invest in innovation. However, these investments must be justified. It has not been made clear to the committee if S&T has a system to monitor research milestones and collect feedback from customers and end-users on the effectiveness of the services delivered by the directorate.

There have to be metrics to justify how S&T develops security solutions. Mr. Under Secretary, you and I both know the importance of innovation, and we have actually talked about it. The next technology that could advance the Department's goal could be in the hands of a small business owner. Unfortunately, there have been instances where small companies complain about their difficulty in working with S&T. I hope to hear the strategy the director has to improve its relationship with small and/or minority-owned businesses.

Mr. Chairman, I hope the committee will take these matters seriously as we learn how the directorate will carry out its strategic plans, management directives, and operational programs going forward.

Thank you, and I yield back.

Mr. MEEHAN. I thank the gentleman. We are also similarly grateful for having the presence of the Ranking Member, another Ranking Member, and the Chairman of the full Science, Space, and Technology Committee, the gentleman from Texas, Mr. Smith. Thank you for being here.

I recognize you for any opening comment you may have.

Mr. SMITH. Thank you, Mr. Chairman. Thank you, Mr. Chairman—both Chairs who are here today—for having this joint hearing. Today, we have an opportunity to continue our discussion about the work of the Department of Homeland Security's Science and Technology Directorate. In July, the Science Committee's Research and Technology and Oversight Subcommittees held a hearing on technologies that would help secure the border. At that hearing, witnesses discussed the need for a unified strategy and consistent metrics for developing border technologies.

As with other Department components, the Science and Technology Directorate has yet to provide the necessary strategy and technology to control our Nation's borders. A Nation that has lost control of its border has lost control of its future. The Government Accountability Office found the Department of Homeland Security's research and development efforts to be, "fragmented and overlapping." In previous years, the GAO found hundreds of millions of dollars being spent each year on duplicative R&D projects by other offices within the Department.

The Science and Technology Directorate will spend $1.2 billion this year on numerous projects. The Science and Technology Directorate is uniquely positioned to interact with all of DHS components. It not only is in a position to help secure our physical border, but also can better protect our virtual borders related to network and information technology.

I am particularly interested in learning about the directorate's work on cybersecurity issues. Dr. Brothers and his team have made cybersecurity a centerpiece of their recently-released visionary goals.

On a daily basis, our Nation's economy and security are threatened by cyber criminals and hackers. Unfriendly foreign governments launch regular cyber attacks to undermine our National security and steal military and technological secrets. Cyber attacks against U.S. Government and private-sector networks continue to grow at an alarming rate. But the full scope of the threat we face has yet to be realized. Unfortunately, the Senate continues to sit on numerous bills passed by the House that would make our cyber infrastructure more secure.

Many of these bills were initiated by the Science, Space, and Technology Committee and the Homeland Security Committee. While the Senate remains immobile, we will continue our work on solutions here in the House. Unsecure physical and virtual borders threaten our National and economic security. Technology can help us better secure our borders and determine our future. I look forward to hearing from our witnesses today and want, again, to thank our Chairmen for conducting this hearing.

I will yield back.

[The statement of Chairman Smith follows:]

STATEMENT OF CHAIRMAN LAMAR S. SMITH

SEPTEMBER 9, 2014

Thank you, Chairman Meehan and Chairman Bucshon for holding this joint hearing. Today we have an opportunity to continue our discussion about the work of the Department of Homeland Security's Science and Technology Directorate.

In July, the Science, Space, and Technology Committee's Research and Technology and Oversight Subcommittees held a hearing on technologies that would help to secure the border.

At that hearing, witnesses discussed the need for a unified strategy and consistent metrics for developing border technologies.

As with other Department components, the Science and Technology Directorate has yet to provide the necessary strategy and technology to control our Nation's borders. A Nation that has lost control of its border has lost control of its future.

The Government Accountability Office (GAO) found the Department of Homeland Security's (DHS's) research and development (R&D) efforts to be "fragmented and overlapping."

In previous years, the GAO found hundreds of millions of dollars being spent each year on duplicative R&D projects by other offices within the Department. The Science and Technology Directorate will spend $1.2 billion this year on numerous projects.

The Science and Technology Directorate is uniquely positioned to interact with all of DHS's components. It not only is in a position to help secure our physical border, but also can better protect our virtual borders related to network and information technology.

I am particularly interested in learning about the Directorate's work on cybersecurity issues. Dr. Brothers and his team have made cybersecurity a centerpiece of their recently-released "visionary goals."

On a daily basis, our Nation's economy and security are threatened by cyber criminals and hackers. Unfriendly foreign goverments launch regular cyber attacks to undermine our National security and steal military and technological secrets.

Cyber attacks against U.S. Government and private-sector networks continue to grow at an alarming rate. But the full scope of the threat we face has yet to be realized.

Unfortunately, the Senate continues to sit on numerous bills passed by the House that would make our cyber infrastructure more secure. Many of these bills were initiated by the Science, Space, and Technology Committee and the Homeland Security Committee.

While the Senate remains immobile, we will continue to work on solutions here in the House. Unsecure physical and virtual borders threaten our National and economic security. Technology can help us better secure our borders and determine our future.

I look forward to hearing from the witnesses today and will continue to work on legislation to set priorities for the Science and Technology Directorate.

Mr. MEEHAN. Let me thank the Chairman. Other Members of the committee: A reminder that opening statements may be submitted for the record.

Mr. MEEHAN. We are pleased to have a distinguished panel of witnesses before us today on this very important topic. Let me begin by introducing Dr. Reginald Brothers. He is the under secretary for science and technology at the Department of Homeland Security. As under secretary, Dr. Brothers is the science advisor to the Secretary and is responsible for oversight and management of Science and Technology Directorate, the Department's primary research and development arm.

Dr. Brothers is a science and technology leader, an expert with more than 20 years of private- and public-sector experience. Prior to joining DHS, Dr. Brothers served as the deputy assistant secretary of defense for research. He was a technical fellow, and director for mission applications at BAE Systems, as well as a program manager for the Defense Advanced Research Projects Agency. Welcome, Dr. Brothers.

We are joined also by Mr. David Maurer. He is the director in the United States Government Accountability Office's Homeland Security and Justice team, where he leads GAO's work reviewing DHS and DOJ management issues. As a former member of the Department of Justice, I remember that oversight. I thank you for your work. His past work includes reports and testimonies on DHS research and development, DOJ grant programs, the Federal prison system, Federal judgeships, DHS morale, and DHS's overseas presence.

The witnesses' full written statements will appear in the record, and I thank you for your extensive written statements that give us a full spectrum on the issues before you. But in the time you have, I hope that you will focus on your priorities, Dr. Brothers.

I look forward to recognizing you for your testimony.

STATEMENT OF REGINALD BROTHERS, UNDER SECRETARY FOR SCIENCE AND TECHNOLOGY, DEPARTMENT OF HOME-LAND SECURITY

Under Secretary BROTHERS. Thank you, and good morning. Chairman Meehan, Chairman Bucshon, Ranking Member Payne, Ranking Member Lipinski, Ranking Member Thompson, Chairman Smith, and distinguished Members of the subcommittees, I want to thank you for this opportunity to discuss the mission and strategy of the Department of Homeland Security Science and Technology Directorate. I would also like to thank the Members of the subcommittees for their long-standing interest in, and support of, science technology, as evidenced recently by legislation such as H.R. 2952 and 33696.

With this reauthorization, the committee has an opportunity to help launch S&T as a 21st Century research and development organization who will serve as a model for Federal R&D; one that is hyper-connected, exploring the convergence of scientific and technical disciplines, capable of meeting increasing demand for return on taxpayer dollars, and tailored to the new digital age. I would like to open with two observations from my 4 months as under secretary.

First, it is apparent that technology and R&D are an essential bridge to the future of homeland security. S&T will be central to helping the Department make that future a reality. Given current and projected threat environments, technology-based solutions will be increasingly relied upon as force multipliers to give operators and first responders the operational advantage. Second, S&T is the right team for the job. It is a dedicated, passionate workforce and solid stakeholder base. Walking the halls and speaking to our partners, I am invigorated by the wide-spread enthusiasm for our mission. They are hungry to contribute, and we have the technical breadth and depth to work with operators and end-users across the full extent of the Department's missions.

Given these two observations, I am optimistic for S&T's future. The objective is to help actualize S&T's potential and make it a full-fledged enabler, innovator, and trusted performer across the Department. To this end, I came to S&T with five priorities: The creation and execution of visionary goals; an actionable strategy; an empowered workforce; force-multiplying solutions; and an energized homeland security industrial base. I am proud to say that even after only 4 months we are well on our way.

Upon my arrival at S&T, I saw visionary goals that would capitalize on creativity, improve transparency and morale, and serve as north stars to drive innovation within S&T and our broader community. R&D requires imagination. We must tap into inventiveness across the entire S&T ecosystem of our laboratories, industry, and academia at home and abroad. I called on all S&T internal personnel and DHS components, stakeholders, end-users, and industry partners to participate in the process and provide their insights.

The visionary goals process has started a National dialogue, one that we plan to continue, that has included 1,500 people participating on-line from industry, academia, and Federal, State, and local entities. But the goals as an ambitious end-state, our next step is the development of a strategic plan for S&T, with a 5-year time horizon. This nearer-term road map will lay out how our organization will achieve our visionary end-goals and determine concrete metrics for success. Upon completion of the S&T strategic plan later this year, I look forward to sharing it with this committee, the rest of Congress, and our stakeholders in industry and academia.

Part of positioning S&T more strategically was shifting our approach to R&D and including more aggressive, higher-potential impact programs. A balanced R&D portfolio makes appropriate trade-offs between technical feasibility and operational impact, weighs threat probability, and appropriately distributes investments across performance types and project time lines. In recent years, S&T has not had this freedom or flexibility. But if we focus entirely on incrementally improving existing technology and systems we won't provide the next generation the leap-ahead solutions our customers need.

To achieve our potential, S&T and our stakeholders need to weigh these trade-offs and balance delivery of both near-term and riskier, longer-term, game-changing capabilities to our end-users. All the strategic planning and portfolio development that we will describe today depends on identification of capability gaps. We will continue refining our process for generating these gaps based on the combination of conceptual development, hands-on experimentation, analysis of future threats and embedding directly with operators. Much of this is already done informally. Some of it, like the embed program, will be new.

To function in this new digital age and to generate capability gaps and usable solutions to these gaps will depend on program managers who can break down firewalls between R&D and operations and become fluent in the language of operators. S&T fills critical roles as the R&D engine of the homeland security enterprise. A reauthorization is an opportunity to shape the R&D organization for the 21st Century and to give S&T the flexibility to empower our workforce, engage more effectively with industry and other non-Government stakeholders, and bring more and better solutions to our DHS and first-responder customers.

Thank you for inviting me today to discuss S&T and share my vision for the directorate. I am thrilled to be part of this organization, and know that with your support in Congress we will continue making great strides in finding new and better ways to support homeland security operations.

I look forward to your questions.

[The prepared statement of Secretary Brothers follows:]

PREPARED STATEMENT OF REGINALD BROTHERS

SEPTEMBER 9, 2014

Good morning Chairman Meehan, Chairman Bucshon, Ranking Member Clark, Ranking Member Lipinski, and distinguished Members of the subcommittees. Thank you for the opportunity to testify before you today on re-authorization of the Department of Homeland Security's (DHS) Science and Technology Directorate (S&T). In this testimony, I will discuss how S&T, one of a handful of components in the Department created from whole cloth under the original Homeland Security Act of 2002, has grown in the last 11 years into a trusted partner for DHS operators and State, local, Tribal, and territorial first responders. With S&T's reauthorization, the committee has an opportunity to help launch a 21st Century research and development (R&D) organization that will serve as a model for Federal R&D—hyper-connected, exploiting the convergence of scientific and technical disciplines, capable of meeting increasing demand for return on taxpayer dollars, and tailored to the new "digital age."[1]

---

[1] A term borrowed from Eric Schmidt and Jared Cohen's *The New Digital Age*, which illustrates potential opportunities and challenges in the emerging technological era that we will inhabit.

To frame the conversation about S&T, I have two observations from my time so far as under secretary. First, I believe given the current and projected threat environments, technology-based solutions (materiel and human-centric) will increasingly be an essential force multiplier to providing operators and first responders the upper hand in their respective operational spaces. Technology and R&D are the bridge to the future of homeland security. For example, without harnessing advances in science and technology, we simply cannot, with current resources, screen and secure continuously rising flows of passengers and cargo and counter sophisticated, motivated adversaries at land, air, and sea Ports of Entry. The most effective and efficient changes come with smart application of technical and analytical expertise. Though S&T's value and capabilities are acknowledged by many throughout the Department, we continue to seek new partners and help address the growing need for technology in the Homeland Security Enterprise.

The second observation is that S&T has a passionate and dedicated workforce. Walking the halls, I am invigorated by the wide-spread enthusiasm for our mission. Our workforce is hungry to contribute, and we have the technical breadth and depth to work with operators and end-users across the breadth of the Department's missions.

I believe that given S&T's workforce and the rising urgency for technology as a force multiplier, there is yet-to-be-realized potential for S&T to support the Department and the Nation. In the coming years, my objective is to help S&T actualize that potential and become a full-fledged enabler and trusted performer across the Department. This pursuit, and the ability for S&T to provide the bridge between present and future homeland security capabilities, rest significantly on whether we can transform the directorate into a 21st Century Federal R&D organization. For that, we need help from Congress.

As under secretary, my thinking is influenced by lessons learned in my time at the Department of Defense (DoD), in industry, and at Federally-funded laboratories. Many corporate labs today are under increased pressure to prove a direct impact to profits. Some laboratories are seen by business unit leaders as imposing an unjustified tax, and many surviving laboratories ensure that their researchers have at minimum a baseline understanding of the business context of their work. One way that these laboratories are enabling this understanding is by cycling researchers between business units and work in the lab. This is a straightforward, deceptively simple-sounding concept, but it can make the difference between a lab disconnected from its customers and one ultimately providing a strong return on investment and expanding business through attunement to operational reality and generation of usable, imaginative solutions. This is precisely the model I intend to implement at S&T with DHS's operational components.

After my confirmation, I came to S&T with five priorities to execute—*visionary goals, actionable strategy, an empowered workforce, force multiplying solutions, and an energized Homeland Security Industrial Base*—to address how we plan as a directorate and to ensure that we fully leverage all available resources. As I see it, there are opportunities to further refine and improve how we work and what we focus on as an organization. Those priorities split into two basic categories: First, how we plan and prioritize at S&T and, second, how to bring all available resources to bear in execution of our programs.

It is important to mention one item to provide additional strategic context before covering specifics. To address the range of challenges the Nation faces most collaboratively and effectively within the Department, we have recently undertaken an initiative entitled "Strengthening Departmental Unity of Effort." In his April 22, 2014, memorandum, Secretary Johnson directed a series of actions to enhance the cohesiveness of the Department, while preserving the professionalism, skill, and dedication of the people within, and the rich history of, the DHS components.

There are two elements in this initiative: New senior leader forums led by the Secretary and the Deputy, and Department-wide strategy, requirements, and budget development and acquisition processes that are tied to strategic guidance and informed by joint operational plans and joint operations. These are building and maturing DHS into an organization that is greater than the sum of its parts—one that operates much more collaboratively, leverages shared strengths, realizes shared efficiencies, and allows us to further improve our important role as an effective domestic and international partner. DHS S&T participates fully in the range of Unity of Effort initiative activities directed by the Secretary, but just as significantly, functions as a directorate with the same unifying principles.

A STRATEGIC FOCUS FOR HOMELAND SECURITY

Effective planning is how we as an organization will translate the basis for our work (e.g., Component priorities, the Secretary's initiatives, Congressional mandates, White House policy) into functional programs that ultimately deliver novel or improved capability. This includes a strategic vision spanning the near term, including specific courses of action, through the long term and far horizon, including ambitious goals.

Four Visionary Goals

As a first step, one of my priorities coming on-board was establishing visionary goals that would serve as 30-year horizon points to build toward. When Dr. George Heilmeier, one of the great technology leaders of our time, was director of the Defense Advanced Research Projects Agency, the organization and its stakeholders were invigorated by his articulation of visionary goals, what he called his "silver bullets." *Make the oceans transparent. Create an invisible aircraft.* Heilmeier's visionary goals strove for previously-unachieved capabilities and lower-cost equivalents to existing capabilities. They helped orient the organization and inspired stakeholders, including operators, end-users, and performers in industry and academia.

R&D requires creativity and imagination, and we must tap into that enthusiasm to spur big thinking. At S&T, I tasked a working group with representatives from throughout the organization to draft vision statements for consumption and feedback from the rest of the directorate and our end-user stakeholders. Building off of existing policy and doctrine (e.g., the Quadrennial Homeland Security Review, Secretary Johnson's priorities, existing Homeland Security Presidential Directives), the group generated the four following draft goals:

- *Screening at Speed: Matching the Pace of Life.*—Noninvasive screening at speed will provide for comprehensive threat protection while adapting security to the pace of life rather than life to security. Whether screening people, baggage, or cargo, unobtrusive technologies and improved processes will enable the seamless detection of threats while respecting privacy, with minimal impact to the speed of travel and the pace of commerce.
- *A Trusted Cyber Future: Protecting Privacy, Commerce, and Community.*—In a future of increasing cyber connections, users will trust that infrastructure is resilient, information is protected, illegal use is deterred, and privacy is not compromised. Frictionless security will operate seamlessly in the background, based on self-detecting, self-protecting, and self-healing cyber critical infrastructure—all without disruption.
- *Enable the Decision Maker: Providing Actionable Information Ahead of Incident Speed.*—The decision maker has improved situational awareness and is better able to understand risks, weigh options, and take action—literally experience the information. The essential element to making informed decisions is access to timely, accurate, context-based information. Supported by new decision support, modeling, and simulation systems, critical decisions can be made based on relevant information, transforming disparate data into proactive wisdom, and ultimately improving operational effectiveness.
- *Responder of the Future: Protected, Connected, and Fully Aware.*—The responder of the future is threat-adaptive, able to respond to all dangers safely and effectively. Armed with comprehensive physical protection; interoperable, networked tools; technology-enhanced threat detection and mitigation capabilities; and timely, actionable information, the responder of the future will be able to serve more safely and effectively as an integral part of the Nation's resiliency.

Following the development of the initial draft set of visionary goals by the working group, we opened them to Directorate-wide discussion and development. Based on that feedback, changes were made before a second wave of input from a wider group including the Department and external stakeholders outside DHS.

One important note is that these are our visionary goals, but they certainly do not capture our R&D portfolio in its entirety. The homeland security mission space is broad, and many critical efforts are not or are only indirectly included in these goals. That a particular current effort is not captured in a 30-year vision does not necessarily speak to the value of a potential project or place within S&T's portfolio of investments. The visionary goals are devices to capitalize on creativity and serve as North Stars to drive innovation within S&T and our broader community.

An Actionable Strategy

With the visionary goals as an ambitious end-state, the next step is a narrower, 5- to 10-year strategic plan for S&T. This will be a nearer-term roadmap for how our organization seeks to achieve our visionary end goals. Development of a strategy is a platform to think through and communicate our plan internally and, as a result, make the most of our investments. Externally, a good strategy also provides critical signposts to industry, Congress, and other stakeholders for where our priorities lie and the path we seek to reach for long-time horizon deliverables. This is a standard tool in industry and elsewhere. I look forward to using the same approach at S&T to make us more accessible and to be the foundation for how we interface within the Department, as an interagency partner, and with industry and our other non-Federal partners.

Drawing on my experience in industry, a strategic plan must be actionable and, in order to be useful, cannot simply be a reiteration of our existing work and tally of our investments over the last 5 years projected into the future. We need to lay out S&T's next 5 to 10 years and determine concrete metrics for success. In order to keep the strategy current and account for unanticipated changes or emergent priorities, the strategy will also be revisited as part of a periodic process. Upon completion of the S&T Strategic Plan later this year, I look forward to sharing it with this committee, the rest of Congress, and our stakeholders in industry and academia at home and abroad.

Delivering Force-Multiplying Solutions

In order to position the directorate more strategically, we are updating our approach to R&D programs. A new approach will allow a more focused, strategic relationship with our partners and will address the need for a jointly-calibrated investment risk profile. At times, there will rightly be pressure to fill immediate needs or invest in incremental improvements, but a healthy portfolio must still allow for a portion of projects to carry more technical risk and offer proportionally greater potential returns. My vision for a balanced R&D portfolio is one that makes appropriate trade-offs between technical feasibility and operational impact of projects, weighs potential event's probability and impact, and that distributes appropriately across types of performers (including non-traditional) and project time lines (less than 1 year vs. 5 years).

As such, I plan for a portfolio that spans quick success projects integrating off-the-shelf technologies to potentially disruptive technologies that, out of necessity, will be high-risk. S&T and our stakeholders have to embrace the risk-capability trade-offs if we are to achieve our potential to deliver both near-term and game-changing capabilities to our end-users. There will also be three categories of programs, outlined below, that will ultimately reduce S&T's total number of programs but will increase overall impact, strategic focus, and sustainability of the R&D portfolio.

The first category will be our Apex programs. Since S&T's first Apex began with the Secret Service in 2010, Apex programs have been some of our most successful and have generated a full range of lessons learned including on front-end assessment and capability baselining, working jointly with DHS operational partners, and joint program execution. Much of the original Apex structure will remain—these will still be cross-cutting, multi-disciplinary efforts intended to solve problems of strategic operational importance—but the projects are being scaled to apply to a wider portion of the portfolio and will operate on longer 5-year time lines. The new Apexes will include some current projects rolled up with expanded or new ones. With high-profile programs, concrete deliverables, precise milestones and time lines, and significant increases in dollar and workforce investment, we believe that the new, scaled Apex efforts will bring substantial gains for our operational partners involved with screening, cyber security, flood resilience, biodetection, and emergency response.

The second category of programs will be what we currently refer to as our Technology Engine programs. These will focus on technology foraging and the development of specific core capabilities and systems that cut across, and benefit, numerous programs and projects across S&T's portfolio. We see these bringing a push-pull dynamic to the directorate. They will be pulled as service providers to Apexes and other efforts (e.g., numerous programs have data analytic or network security needs), but they will also push for integration of universal needs and capabilities like interoperability into projects throughout S&T. These technology areas, including data analytics or modeling and simulation as examples, will provide a critical mass of knowledge and expertise to ensure efficiency and proper leverage of previous, current, and future investments.

The final category includes many focused programs not captured under the umbrella of Apexes or Technology Engines but which are still critical for meeting the needs of DHS components and our Homeland Security Enterprise partners. Example programs would include our development of bioassays, which are a foundational element of the Nation's biodefense and ability to screen and monitor for pathogens and potential bio-attacks. This would also include investments in research infrastructure and unique testbeds such as our cyber experimental research testbed, which allows cybersecurity researchers to test and refine their tools and technologies in large, internet-scale conditions.

S&T's Process for Identifying Capability Gaps

There are two elements of S&T's work that are complementary but distinct. The first, requirements, is for acquisition programs and deals with physical characteristics and operational necessities (e.g., weight, dimension, ruggedness, look and feel). S&T's contributions in this area include participation in the Department's joint capabilities and requirements process. Operational capability gaps, which are the second element, address missions, or subsets of missions that cannot be met currently or efficiencies which significantly enhance performance; these are based on customer and end-user input. These operational capability gaps serve as S&T's primary driver for what we focus on in R&D programs.

Regarding requirements, as you know, the Secretary established a Department-wide Joint Requirements Council (JRC) in June as part of his Unity of Effort Initiative. The JRC identifies common capability needs and challenges across DHS components, and will work as an essential input into S&T's own R&D process. In addition to JRC membership, S&T currently provides the JRC's primary analytic resources. As such, S&T is helping develop and refine JRC analysis, methodology, and process in addition to partnering with topic-specific teams to conduct capabilities-based assessments. Working under the direction of the JRC Chair and with the other JRC stakeholders, we will establish a lasting and functional framework for the Department's requirements process.

The JRC and corresponding DHS joint requirements process often highlight capability gaps and can generate valuable input for S&T's programs. However, acquisition-related input like physical requirements is not the primary basis for R&D programs. For a successful R&D organization, any programs, strategy, or visionary goals ultimately must grow from and be tied to customers' and end-users' capability gaps. A healthy process for identifying capability gaps is an R&D organization's engine for understanding what our stakeholders need to do their jobs, for knowing where and what services to provide (e.g., later-stage acquisition support, engineering services, subject-matter expertise), and for validating the effectiveness and the value of the investments that S&T is making.

Moving forward, S&T will formalize and integrate its framework for communicating, documenting, addressing, and reviewing capability gaps and R&D requirements. These generally grow from two complementary categories. The first is conceptual development through embedding directly with operators, analysis of future threats, or other interaction with operators. The second is through hands-on experimentation, also influenced by embedding with operators as well as through types of events like those in the Joint Interagency Field Exploration program.[2] Those R&D requirements will then be the basis for S&T's technology roadmaps and new start programs.

There are several driving principles as S&T locks in its formal process for identifying capability gaps: Top-down prioritization by leadership; bottom-up engagement with operational staff and end-users for challenge statements, proposals, and validation; documents capturing current efforts, challenges, and strategies; and periodic engagement and review at both the executive and working levels of our organizations. Though this process will feature many of the same elements across our many partner organizations, it will be tailored to each customer in order to ensure functional governance, appropriate resource commitment, and mutual management of expectations.

A 21st Century R&D Workforce

Going back to the lessons learned from corporate labs that have maintained their value to organizations, I look forward to implementation of a much more robust process for S&T's workforce to embed with operators and to allow operational staff to detail to S&T and provide direct input to our R&D projects. To function in the new digital age, we need scientists who break down firewalls between R&D and op-

---

[2] Sponsored by S&T and the Department of Defense and conducted in conjunction with the Naval Postgraduate School, Joint Interagency Field Exploration events bring together operational end-users with technology companies to explore the potential of new capabilities to address challenges faced by Federal agencies. The environment facilitates a collaborative working relationship between Government, academia, industry, and non-Governmental organizations to promote the identification and assessment of emerging and maturing technologies with the primary goal of accelerating the delivery of enhanced capabilities to the end-user.

erations and who become fluent in the language of operators and end-users. These "multi-lingual" program managers that can slide between operational and technical environments have the best track records for successful projects and transition to use.

To achieve this, I would like more opportunities for staff to gain first-hand understanding of DHS operations through a formal program to embed technical subject-matter expertise experts in the field with operators. We will have different durations for different purposes and outcomes, perhaps a 2-week speed embed in some cases and in others a more comprehensive 6-month or 1-year stint. There are considerable obstacles to overcome in order to successfully launch such a program—e.g., ensuring staff embed in the right places and see real operations, that staff are in a position that does not disrupt law enforcement or other sensitive operations—but the benefit of deeper connection to customers and a reinforced R&D requirements process speak for themselves.

I also believe that achieving this adaptable, "multi-lingual" workforce requires a more agile and modern hiring authority that is suited to an R&D organization. Part of being responsive to end-user R&D requirements is agility and adaptability in our workforce. This implies that our program managers are able to work across the three categories of programs detailed above and have skill sets that are not limited to a specific line of business or type of project. That also means being able to boost our talented career workforce with more strategic use of our existing hiring authorities in the Homeland Security Act to fill urgent needs and inject outside perspective into our programs. With a fluid workforce strengthened through term-limited outside hires, our external S&T stakeholders are more effectively connected to the organization, we can foster technical engagement (including with STEM students) on homeland security challenges, and our organization is better-positioned to support the Department and first responders.

LEVERAGING ALL AVAILABLE RESOURCES

In addition to more effective planning, we are also working to ensure that S&T takes advantage of the full spectrum of resources across what I refer to as the S&T ecosystem, which is the broad network of technical expertise inside and outside of Government that can be brought to bear for virtually any issue operators face. This S&T ecosystem includes Department of Energy and DoD labs that are National assets and global leaders in many research areas; our Nation's broad base of universities, many of which are DHS Centers of Excellence; and small businesses, the heart of our Nation's innovation, that we engage through specialized vehicles like our Small Business Innovation Research (SBIR) awards. Any potential R&D performer inside and outside Government across industry, academia, Government-funded and private laboratories, and in the United States or abroad is a part of the S&T Ecosystem.

The Federal Government no longer provides the same share of funding for research and development as it did in the Cold War era, and we can no longer assume we have access to the best minds if we work exclusively through who and what we already know.[3] Though it is easy to stovepipe and use known performers, a 21st Century R&D organization must tap innovation engines in the venture capital world, Silicon Valley, or universities to name a few. We face a vast homeland security threat space and the entire Homeland Security Enterprise benefits from a wider base of potential performers engaged in homeland security R&D. The more vehicles to reach those potential performers (including DHS Centers of Excellence and SBIR above, cooperative research and development agreements, newly-delegated prize authority, and so on), the more effectively and efficiently we can develop essential security solutions.

An Empowered S&T Workforce

Tapping the full potential of the S&T ecosystem will require putting effort into improving coordination and collaboration within DHS S&T. Across offices at S&T, we already cover most of the S&T Ecosystem on a piece-by-piece basis with several offices actively engaged with innovative potential performers. We can be doing more, however, to ensure that S&T is internally unified and using those connections toward a common purpose. I will foster an even greater Unity of Effort between elements of S&T like the Homeland Security Advanced Research Projects Agency, our university-based Centers of Excellence, our five operational homeland security labs,

---

[3] The Federal Government was the main provider of the Nation's R&D accounting for 53.9 percent in 1953 and 66.8 percent in 1964. In 2011, Federal spending accounted for 29.6% of the Nation's R&D spending. Source: National Science Foundation (*http://www.nsf.gov/statistics/seind14/content/chapter-4/at04-06.pdf*).

our Acquisition Support and Operations Analysis group, or our Small Business Innovation Research program. That will allow S&T to tailor our R&D portfolio performers to those suited to greater innovation or greater feasibility based on mission needs and demands.

Having that type of agile, cross-connected, and empowered workforce means recognizing the value of taking a risk if the payout is a disruptive capability, such as total situational awareness at all land borders. In recent years, DHS S&T has not had this freedom or flexibility. But for the long-term health of DHS and the Homeland Security Enterprise, S&T and its stakeholders must be tolerant of more risk in S&T's R&D portfolio. We will still pursue lower-risk, more incremental projects where appropriate. But we will also foster innovation at S&T with institutional allowance for more risky projects that carry higher potential of failure but also significant potential for reward if the project succeeds. An R&D organization is not fulfilling its mission if it focuses on minor improvements to the last great thing at the cost of failing to pursue the next great thing; we must balance our workforce and our investments against that.

An Energized Homeland Security Industrial Base

Another aspect of leveraging the full S&T ecosystem is fostering deeper engagement with an energized Homeland Security Industrial Base. The Department of Defense has the Defense Industrial Base, a private-sector engine for design, production, and maintenance of our military's weapons and systems. When Defense needs a new missile, submarine, or communications network, industrial machinery outside of Government develops and delivers a product. While DHS cannot match the DoD's resources, I know from my time in industry that companies of all sizes are interested in doing business in homeland security.

Our Department, similar to much of Government, is often criticized by industry for lack of transparency and failure to share information to help private companies align their own investments to where Government needs help. S&T will proactively address these criticisms. I have already noted some instances—an updated and actionable S&T Strategic Plan tailored to companies, a refined R&D requirements process, more effective outreach and information sharing, and a more transparent and informative web presence. My hope as under secretary is, through sustained and effective engagement with the Homeland Security Industrial Base, that we begin to see industry more closely align their internal R&D budgets to homeland security priorities.

S&T'S VALUE TO THE DEPARTMENT

Before I conclude, I think it is important to recognize that, although R&D is the backbone of our organization, S&T has more responsibilities and provides many more services to the Department than a traditional R&D organization. We coordinate and oversee operational test and evaluation for all major investments across DHS. We oversee implementation of the Support Anti-Terrorism by Fostering Effective Technologies Act of 2002, better known as the SAFETY Act, one of the more innovative approaches to incentivizing private development of homeland security-focused technology and services. With the DHS Office of the General Counsel, we are responsible for the entire Department's intellectual property portfolio. We work with all elements of the Department to ensure DHS compliance with treaties such as the Biological Weapons Convention. We operate laboratories, such as the National Biodefense Analysis and Countermeasures Center and Plum Island Animal Disease Center, whose missions extend beyond R&D to supporting operational homeland security missions. We provide technical support that backstops major Departmental initiatives such as end-to-end acquisition reform as part of the Secretary's Strengthening Departmental Unity of Effort initiative. The list goes on.

Because of that wider role, and because our R&D work already connects us with operators throughout the Department, we are one of the elements of DHS that can serve as glue between operational elements. It is critical we preserve this and continue to be viewed as an objective arbiter and trusted partner, not an overseer or disrupter of operations. As this committee contemplates potential new authorities for S&T, please be mindful of this important dynamic. Achieving S&T's mission, bringing technology to the fore for components and first responders, supporting the Secretary's vision for the Department, and fulfilling our Congressional mandates rest largely on being able to leverage a positive relationship with our partners and end-users.

CONCLUSION

Your commitment to S&T's re-authorization validates the role the organization has grown into at DHS and is an important step to shedding the role R&D organizations often fall into today as bill payers for other shorter-term needs. Technology will be essential for answering the challenges we face in homeland security today, and S&T has a critical role to fill as the R&D engine of the Homeland Security Enterprise.

I share a vision for the directorate to help highlight areas where we need your help. S&T today, through considerable work and dedication from its workforce, has made the most of an Industrial Age toolbox in a Digital Age R&D landscape. Re-authorization of S&T is a chance to empower an R&D organization for the 21st Century and to give us the flexibility to empower our workforce, engage more effectively with industry and other non-Government stakeholders, and bring more and better solutions to our DHS and first responder customers.

Thank you for inviting me today to discuss S&T and share my vision for the directorate. I am thrilled to be a part of this organization and know that, with your support in Congress, we will continue making great strides and finding new and better ways to support homeland security operators. I look forward to your questions.

Mr. MEEHAN. Thank you, Dr. Brothers.

The Chairman now recognizes Mr. Maurer for your testimony.

STATEMENT OF DAVID C. MAURER, DIRECTOR, HOMELAND SECURITY AND JUSTICE, U.S. GOVERNMENT ACCOUNTABILITY OFFICE

Mr. MAURER. Good morning, Chairman Meehan, Chairman Bucshon, Chairman Smith, Ranking Member Thompson, Ranking Member Lipinski, Ranking Member Payne, and other Members and staff. I am pleased to be here today to discuss—I got everybody, that is good. I am pleased to be here today to discuss how the findings from GAO's recent work can help the Science and Technology Directorate position itself for the future.

Every year, the taxpayers provide DHS over a billion dollars to support research and development. For that reason alone, the Department needs to ensure its R&D activities work as planned. R&D is also a crucial tool for helping DHS better execute its various missions. At the same time, R&D is inherently risky. Some projects will fail. S&T faces the challenge of striking the right balance between helping end-users meet their mission needs, while also taking informed risks to push the boundaries of science.

In recent years, we found that S&T has made important strides in taking a more strategic approach and tightening its links with the rest of DHS. S&T's coordination with DHS operational components is especially important. None of S&T's ideas and work will see real-world use without working closely with eventual end-users. In that regard, S&T's focus on tightening collaboration with the components is a promising sign. With that said, S&T clearly has a lot of work ahead to bring coherence and structure to its research and development efforts.

Our work identified three key areas for improvement. We found that S&T needs to define R&D, do a better job tracking R&D, and improve how it coordinates R&D. In September 2012, we found a lot of activity across the Department that could be considered research and development. By law, S&T is responsible for overseeing and coordinating all of it. But they can't do that if the various DHS components aren't working from the same definition and agree on what should be coordinated.

Our work also found problems in DHS' efforts to centrally track R&D. The Department struggled to answer basic questions, such as: How much are you spending, what projects are currently under way, and do completed projects meet the needs of their customers? For example, we found that DHS did not know how much its components invested in R&D. That makes it difficult to oversee activities across the Department.

Our work also identified problems in coordination. Now, S&T coordinates with components in may different ways at may different levels. The problem is, some of these mechanisms need to work better and, in some cases, new approaches are needed.

Specifically, the report we issued last year found that S&T lacked a formal process to follow up with the end-users of its deliverables. S&T customers were also much more likely to report that S&T's work did not meet end-user needs. In some instances, we were unable to locate an end-user for an S&T project. So what does this mean for the future? Looking down the road, it will be important for S&T to take action in three areas.

First and foremost, we would like to see S&T and the Department fully implement the recommendations from our prior reports. DHS had recently issued a definition of R&D, and that is a good first step. We look forward to action on our other recommendations that will help S&T track and coordinate R&D activities. Those are important building blocks for the second action: Developing an updated strategy to guide S&T's future direction. Not just what it wants to do, but why and how it will be accomplished in a time of tight budget constraints. As we heard, S&T is currently working on this, which is encouraging. We look forward to seeing the results.

Third, S&T needs a motivated and engaged workforce to carry out its mission. Unfortunately, last year, before Dr. Brothers was under secretary, S&T ranked 299 out of 300 Federal entities in the best places to work rankings. Understanding and addressing the root causes of low morale will help support successful implementation of any changes in strategic direction.

S&T has an important role to play in identifying and filling gaps in technological capacities at DHS. Implementing GAO's recommendations, updating the strategic plan, and addressing morale issues will better position S&T to translate state-of-the-art science into usable tools that help enhance homeland security.

That concludes my opening remarks. Thank you for the opportunity to testify this morning. I look forward to your questions.

[The prepared statement of Mr. Maurer follows:]

PREPARED STATEMENT OF DAVID C. MAURER

SEPTEMBER 9, 2014

GAO HIGHLIGHTS

Highlights of GAO–14–865T, a testimony before the Cybersecurity, Infrastructure Protection, and Security Technologies Subcommittee of the Homeland Security Committee and the Research and Technology Subcommittee of the Science, Space, and Technology Committee, House of Representatives.

Why GAO Did This Study

Conducting R&D on technologies for detecting, preventing, and mitigating terrorist threats is vital to enhancing the security of the Nation. Since its creation,

DHS has spent billions of dollars researching and developing technologies used to support its missions. Within DHS, S&T conducts and is responsible for coordinating R&D across the Department. Other components also conduct R&D to support their respective missions.

This statement discusses: (1) How much DHS invests in R&D and the extent to which DHS has policies and guidance for defining and overseeing its R&D efforts across the Department, (2) the extent to which R&D is coordinated across DHS, and (3) the results of DHS border and maritime security R&D efforts and the extent to which DHS has obtained and evaluated feedback on these efforts. This statement is based on GAO's previously-issued work from September 2012 to July 2014, and selected updates conducted in September 2014 on the status of GAO's prior recommendations. To conduct the updates, GAO reviewed agency documentation.

What GAO Recommends

In its prior reports, GAO recommended, among other things, that DHS develop policies and guidance for defining, overseeing, coordinating, and tracking R&D activities across the Department, and that S&T establish time frames and milestones for collecting and evaluating feedback from its customers. DHS concurred with GAO's recommendations and has actions underway to address them.

DEPARTMENT OF HOMELAND SECURITY.—ACTIONS NEEDED TO STRENGTHEN
MANAGEMENT OF RESEARCH AND DEVELOPMENT

What GAO Found

In September 2012, GAO reported that the Department of Homeland Security (DHS) did not know the total amount its components had invested in research and development (R&D) and did not have policies and guidance for defining R&D and overseeing R&D resources across the Department. According to DHS, its Science and Technology Directorate (S&T), Domestic Nuclear Detection Office (DNDO), and Coast Guard were the only components that conducted R&D, and GAO found that these were the only components that reported budget authority, obligations, or outlays for R&D activities to the Office of Management and Budget. However, GAO identified an additional $255 million in R&D obligations made by other DHS components. At the time of GAO's review, DHS did not have a Department-wide policy defining R&D or guidance directing components how to report all R&D activities. GAO recommended that DHS develop policies and guidance to assist components in better understanding how to report R&D activities and better position DHS to determine R&D investments. DHS concurred with the recommendation and, as of September 2014, had updated its guidance to include a definition of R&D but efforts to develop a process for coordinating R&D with other offices remain on-going and have not yet been completed. GAO will continue to monitor DHS's efforts to develop its approach for overseeing R&D at the Department.

GAO also reported in September 2012 that S&T had taken some steps to coordinate R&D efforts across DHS, but the Department's R&D efforts were fragmented and overlapping, a fact that increased the risk of unnecessary duplication. GAO recommended that DHS develop a policy defining roles and responsibilities for coordinating R&D and establish a mechanism to track all R&D projects to help DHS mitigate existing fragmentation and overlap and reduce the risk of unnecessary duplication. DHS concurred with the recommendation. As of September 2014, S&T has not fully implemented new policy guidance but, according to S&T, is conducting portfolio reviews across the Department, as directed by the fiscal year 2013 appropriations act, aimed at coordinating R&D activities. GAO will continue to monitor DHS's efforts to develop a policy to better coordinate and track R&D activities at the Department.

In September 2013, GAO reported that DHS border and maritime R&D components reported producing 97 R&D deliverables from fiscal years 2010 through 2012 at an estimated cost of $177 million. GAO found that the type of border and maritime R&D deliverables produced by S&T, the Coast Guard, and DNDO varied, and R&D customers GAO met with had mixed views on the impact of the deliverables. These deliverables included knowledge products and reports, technology prototypes, and software. For example, S&T developed prototype radar and video systems for use by Border Patrol. However, GAO reported that S&T had not established time frames and milestones for collecting and evaluating feedback on the extent to which deliverables met customers' needs. GAO recommended that S&T establish time frames and milestones for collecting and evaluating such feedback from its customers to better determine the usefulness and impact of its R&D projects and make better-informed decisions regarding future work. As of September 2014, DHS had taken steps to address this recommendation, including making plans to gather customer feedback on a more consistent basis. GAO will continue to monitor DHS's efforts in this area.

Chairman Meehan, Chairman Buschon, Ranking Member Clarke, Ranking Member Lipinski, and Members of the committees: I appreciate the opportunity to testify today about the results of the Department of Homeland Security's (DHS) research and development (R&D) efforts, including the extent to which its R&D efforts are coordinated within and beyond DHS and the results of DHS's border and maritime security R&D efforts. According to the Office of Management and Budget (OMB), R&D activities comprise creative work undertaken on a systematic basis in order to increase the stock of knowledge, including knowledge of man, culture, and society, and the use of this stock of knowledge to devise new applications.[1] R&D is further broken down into the categories of basic research, applied research, and development.[2]

Conducting R&D on technologies for detecting, preventing, and mitigating terrorist threats is vital to enhancing the security of the Nation. DHS, through its Science and Technology Directorate (S&T) and other components, conducts research, development, testing, and evaluation of new technologies that are intended to achieve a range of homeland security goals, including detecting and preventing the unauthorized entry of persons or contraband into the United States; strengthening efforts to prevent and respond to nuclear, biological, explosive, and other types of attacks; and securing U.S. ports and inland waterways. DHS S&T has responsibility for coordinating and integrating all R&D activities of the Department, as provided by the Homeland Security Act of 2002.[3] S&T has five technical divisions responsible for managing the directorate's R&D portfolio and coordinating with other DHS components to identify R&D priorities and needs. Among those divisions, the Borders and Maritime Security Division (BMD) is responsible for most of S&T's border- and maritime-related R&D, and its primary DHS customer is Customs and Border Protection (CBP). Also within S&T, the Office of University Programs manages the DHS Centers of Excellence, which constitute a network of universities that conduct research for DHS component agencies, with two centers dedicated specifically to border and maritime R&D.

Although S&T conducts R&D and has responsibility for coordinating R&D, other DHS components, including the Domestic Nuclear Detection Office (DNDO) and the U.S. Coast Guard, conduct R&D in support of their respective missions. DNDO, for example, conducts R&D related to detecting the use of an unauthorized nuclear explosive device, fissile material, or radiological material in the United States.[4] The U.S. Coast Guard's R&D efforts support all of the various Coast Guard missions, such as search and rescue, migrant interdiction, and marine safety.

Since it began operations in 2003, DHS, through both S&T and other components, has spent billions of dollars researching and developing technologies used to support a wide range of missions. In June 2009, the National Academy of Public Administration (NAPA) reported on S&T's structure, processes, and the execution of its cross-Government leadership role.[5] NAPA reported that although S&T was charged by statute to provide a leading role in guiding homeland-security-related research, S&T has no authority over other Federal agencies that conduct homeland-security-related research, and that the weaknesses in S&T's strategic planning increased the risk for duplication of efforts. NAPA recommended, among other things, that S&T follow OMB and GAO guidance in formulating a strategic plan to guide its work. In July 2012, S&T provided a draft strategy that identifies the roles and responsibilities for

---

[1] OMB Circular No. A–11 Section 84.4. This definition includes administrative expenses for R&D, but excludes physical assets for R&D (such as R&D equipment and facilities), routine testing, quality control mapping, collection of general-purpose statistics, experimental production, routine monitoring and evaluation of an operational program, and the training of scientific and technical personnel.

[2] According to OMB, basic research is a systematic study directed toward a fuller knowledge or understanding of the fundamental aspects of phenomena and of observable facts without specific applications toward processes or products in mind. Applied research is a systematic study to gain knowledge or understanding to determine the means by which a recognized and specific need may be met. Development is a systematic application of knowledge or understanding, directed toward the production of useful materials, devices, and systems or methods, including design, development, and improvement of prototypes and new processes to meet specific requirements. OMB Circular No. A–11 Section 84.

[3] Pub. L. No. 107–296, § 302 (12), 116 Stat. 2135, 2163–64 (codified as amended at 6 U.S.C. § 182 (12)).

[4] DNDO was established by National Security Presidential Directive 43, Homeland Security Presidential Directive 14, and the Security and Accountability for Every Port Act of 2006 (SAFE Port Act). Pub. L. No. 109–347, § 501(a), 120 Stat. 1884, 1932 (codified at 6 U.S.C. §§ 591–596).

[5] National Academy of Public Administration, *Department of Homeland Security Science and Technology Directorate: Developing Technology to Protect America* (Washington, DC: June 2009).

coordinating homeland security science- and technology-related functions across the U.S. Government to the White House's Office of Science & Technology Policy for review. We reported in July 2013 that the White House had not yet approved that draft.

To report R&D-related spending, DHS uses several mechanisms, including budget authority (the legal authorization to obligate funds), obligations (binding agreements to make a payment for services), and outlays (payments to liquidate obligations representing amount expended). Further, OMB requires agencies to submit data on R&D programs as part of their annual budget submissions on investments for basic research, applied research, development, R&D facilities construction, and major equipment for R&D using OMB's definition of R&D. R&D is further broken down into the categories of basic research, applied research, and development.

My testimony today is based on previously-issued reports and addresses: (1) How much DHS invests in R&D and the extent to which it has policies and guidance for defining R&D and overseeing R&D resources and efforts across the Department; (2) the extent to which R&D is coordinated within DHS to prevent overlap, fragmentation, and unnecessary duplication across the Department; and (3) the results of DHS's border and maritime security R&D and the extent to which DHS obtained and evaluated feedback on these efforts.

This statement is based on our previous reports and testimonies issued from September 2012 to July 2014, with selected updates conducted in September 2014 related to S&T's efforts to better manage and coordinate its border and maritime R&D efforts.[6] To conduct our earlier work, among other things, we analyzed data related to DHS's R&D budget authority for fiscal years 2010 through 2013, R&D contracts issued by components to private industry and universities for fiscal years 2007 through 2011, and the Department of Energy's (DOE) National laboratories from fiscal years 2010 through 2012 to identify how much DHS components obligated for R&D-related work at the National laboratories. We also met with selected R&D project managers and customers. For the selected updates, we reviewed agency documentation on DHS's progress in implementing our prior recommendations. The reports cited provide detailed explanations of our scope and methodology.[7] The work upon which this statement is based was conducted in accordance with generally accepted Government auditing standards. Those standards require that we plan and perform the audit to obtain sufficient, appropriate evidence to provide a reasonable basis for our findings and conclusions based on our audit objectives. We believe that the evidence obtained provides a reasonable basis for our findings and conclusions based on our audit objectives.

DHS DOES NOT KNOW ITS TOTAL INVESTMENT IN R&D, BUT HAS TAKEN SOME STEPS TO UPDATE GUIDANCE

In September 2012, we found that DHS did not know how much its components have invested in R&D, making it difficult to oversee R&D efforts across the Department. According to DHS budget officials, S&T, DNDO, and the U.S. Coast Guard were the only components that conducted R&D, and we found that they were the only components that reported budget authority, obligations, or outlays for R&D activities to OMB as part of the budget process. However, we reported that the data DHS submitted to OMB underreported DHS's R&D obligations because DHS components obligated money for R&D contracts that were not reported to OMB as R&D. Specifically, for fiscal year 2011, we identified an additional $255 million in R&D obligations by other DHS components. These obligations included DHS components providing S&T with funding to conduct R&D on their behalf and components obligating funds through contracts directly to industry, to universities, or with DOE's National laboratories for R&D.

[6] GAO, *Department of Homeland Security: Oversight and Coordination of Research and Development Should Be Strengthened*, GAO–12–837 (Washington, DC: Sept. 12, 2012); *2013 Annual Report: Actions Needed to Reduce Fragmentation, Overlap, and Duplication and Achieve Other Financial Benefits*, GAO–13–279SP (Washington, DC: Apr. 9, 2013); *Department of Homeland Security: Opportunities Exist to Strengthen Efficiency and Effectiveness, Achieve Cost Savings, and Improve Management Functions*, GAO–13–547T (Washington, DC: Apr. 26, 2013); *Government Efficiency and Effectiveness: Opportunities to Reduce Fragmentation, Overlap, and Duplication Through Enhanced Performance Management and Oversight*, GAO–13–590T (Washington, DC: May 22, 2013); *Department of Homeland Security: Opportunities Exist to Better Evaluate and Coordinate Border and Maritime Research and Development*, GAO–13–732 (Washington, DC: Sept. 25, 2013); *Department of Homeland Security: Oversight and Coordination of Research and Development Efforts Could Be Strengthened*, GAO–13–766T (Washington, DC: July 17, 2013); *Department of Homeland Security: Continued Actions Needed to Strengthen Oversight and Coordination of Research and Development*, GAO–14–813T (Washington, DC: July 31, 2014).

[7] GAO–12–837 and GAO–13–732.

Further, we found that the data for fiscal years 2010 through 2013 DHS submitted to OMB also underreported DHS's R&D budget authority and outlays because DNDO did not properly report at least $293 million in R&D budget authority and at least $282 million in R&D outlays.[8] We reported that DHS budget officials agreed that DHS underreported its R&D spending and when asked, could not provide a reason why the omission was not flagged by DHS review.

In addition, in our 2012 report, we found that DHS's R&D budget accounts included a mix of R&D and non-R&D spending. For fiscal year 2011, we estimated that 78 percent of S&T's Research, Development, Acquisition, & Operations account; 51 percent of DNDO's Research, Development, & Operations account; and 43 percent of the Coast Guard's R&D budget account funded R&D activities. As a result, this further complicated DHS's ability to identify its total investment in R&D.

We also reported in September 2012 that DHS did not have a Department-wide policy defining R&D or guidance directing components how to report R&D activities. As a result, we concluded that it was difficult to identify the Department's total investment in R&D, a fact that limited DHS's ability to oversee components' R&D efforts and align them with agency-wide R&D goals and priorities, in accordance with *Standards for Internal Control in the Federal Government.*[9] DHS officials told us at the time that DHS used OMB's definition of R&D, but the definition was broad and its application may not be uniform across components, and thus, R&D investments may not always be identified as R&D. We found that the variation in R&D definitions may contribute to the unreliability of the reporting mechanisms for R&D investments in budget development and execution, as discussed above.

We recommended that DHS develop and implement policies and guidance for defining and overseeing R&D at the Department that include, among other things, a well-understood definition of R&D that provides reasonable assurance that reliable accounting and reporting of R&D resources and activities for internal and external use are achieved. DHS agreed with our recommendation and stated that it planned to evaluate the most effective path forward to guide uniform treatment of R&D across the Department in compliance with OMB rules and was considering a management directive, multicomponent steering committee, or new policy guidance to help better oversee and coordinate R&D. As of September 2014, DHS has updated its guidance to include a definition of R&D, but, as discussed in more detail below, efforts to develop a specific policy outlining R&D roles and responsibilities and a process for overseeing and coordinating R&D with other offices remain on-going and have not yet been completed. We will continue to monitor DHS's efforts to implement these recommendations.

S&T HAS TAKEN SOME ACTIONS TO COORDINATE R&D ACROSS DHS, BUT R&D ACTIVITIES ARE FRAGMENTED AND OVERLAPPING

We reported in September 2012 that the Homeland Security Act of 2002 provides S&T with the responsibility for, among other things, coordinating and integrating all research, development, demonstration, testing, and evaluation activities within DHS and establishing and administering the primary R&D activities of the Department.[10] S&T developed coordination practices that fall into four general categories: (1) S&T component liaisons, (2) R&D agreements between component heads and S&T, (3) joint R&D strategies between S&T and components, and (4) various R&D coordination teams made up of S&T and component project managers, which are discussed in detail in our 2012 report and 2013 testimony.[11]

Despite S&T's efforts to coordinate R&D activities, in September 2012, we reported that R&D at DHS was inherently fragmented because several components within DHS—S&T, the Coast Guard, and DNDO—were each given R&D responsibilities in law, and other DHS components may pursue and conduct their own R&D efforts as long as those activities are coordinated through S&T. Fragmentation among R&D efforts at DHS may be advantageous if the Department determines that it could gain better or faster results by having multiple components engage in

---

[8] At the time of our report, budget figures for fiscal year 2013 were agency estimates.

[9] *Standards for Internal Control in the Federal Government* states that policies and mechanisms are needed to enforce management's directives, such as the process of adhering to requirements for budget development and execution and to ensure the reliability of those and other reports for internal and external use. GAO, *Standards for Internal Control in the Federal Government,* GAO/AIMD–00–21.3.1 (Washington, DC: Nov. 1999).

[10] 6 U.S.C. § 182(11)–(12).

[11] GAO–12–837. GAO, *Department of Homeland Security: Oversight and Coordination of Research and Development Efforts Could be Strengthened,* GAO–13–766T (Washington, DC: July 17, 2013).

R&D activities toward a similar goal; however, it can be disadvantageous if those activities are uncoordinated or unintentionally overlapping or duplicative.

Specifically, we found at least six Department components involved in R&D activities in our review of data on about 15,000 Federal procurement contract actions coded as R&D taken by DHS components from fiscal years 2007 through 2012. We examined 47 R&D contracts awarded by these components—selected because they appeared to have activities similar to those of another contract—and found 35 instances among 29 contracts in which the contracts overlapped with activities conducted elsewhere in the Department. Taken together, these 29 contracts were worth about $66 million. In one example of the overlap, we found that two DHS components awarded 5 separate contracts that each addressed detection of the same chemical.

While we did not identify instances of unnecessary duplication among these contracts, in September 2012, we found that DHS had not developed a policy defining who is responsible for coordinating R&D activities at DHS that could help prevent overlap, fragmentation, or unnecessary duplication and did not have tracking mechanisms or policies to help ensure that overlap is avoided and efforts are better coordinated consistent with *Standards for Internal Control in the Federal Government*.[12] S&T officials told us at the time that a process did not exist at DHS or within S&T to prevent overlap or unnecessary duplication but that relationships with components mitigate that risk. They also stated that S&T has improved interactions with components over time. We concluded that the existence of overlapping R&D activities coupled with the lack of policies and guidance defining R&D and coordination processes was an indication that not all R&D activities at DHS were coordinated to ensure that R&D is not unnecessarily duplicative.

We also found in September 2012 that neither DHS nor S&T tracked all on-going R&D projects across the Department, including R&D activities contracted through the National laboratories. As part of our review, we identified 11 components that reimbursed the National laboratories for R&D from fiscal years 2010 through 2012, but S&T's Office of National Laboratories could not provide us with any information on those activities and told us it did not track them. According to S&T, the Office of National Laboratories' ability to provide information on activities across the Department is limited by components inconsistently operating within the defined process for working with the National laboratories.[13]

As a result, we recommended that DHS develop and implement policies and guidance for overseeing R&D that includes, among other things, a description of the Department's process and roles and responsibilities for overseeing and coordinating R&D investments and efforts, and a mechanism to track existing R&D projects and their associated costs across the Department. DHS agreed with our recommendation and stated at the time that S&T was implementing a collaborative, end-user-focused strategy to coordinate and interact with components to better ensure S&T's efforts aligned with components' needs and that it was considering developing new policy guidance for R&D activities across the Department. According to DHS officials, the Department implemented an R&D portfolio review process, as directed by committee reports accompanying the fiscal year 2013 DHS Appropriations Act, which is aimed at better coordinating R&D activities by reviewing components' individual R&D projects.[14] In April 2014, DHS developed a definition for R&D and stated that S&T was responsible for coordinating and integrating R&D activities throughout the Department. However, as of September 2014, not enough time has passed to determine whether this process and new memorandum have improved coordination. Furthermore, to better define and manage R&D across the Department, DHS should also establish a mechanism to track R&D projects and costs, as we recommended. Fully implementing our recommendation to develop a policy that defines roles and respon-

---

[12] GAO's *Standards for Internal Control in the Federal Government* states that policies and procedures ensure that the necessary activities occur at all levels and functions of the organization—not just from top-level leadership. This ensures that all levels of the organization are coordinating effectively and as part of a larger strategy. Additionally, internal control standards provide that agencies should communicate necessary information effectively by ensuring that they are communicating with, and obtaining information from, external stakeholders that may have a significant impact on the agency achieving its goals.

[13] The Homeland Security Act of 2002 gave DHS the authority to use DOE laboratories to conduct R&D and established S&T's Office of National Laboratories (ONL) to be responsible for coordinating and using the DOE National laboratories. Pub. L. No. 107–296, § 309, 116 Stat. 2135, 2172 (2002) (codified at 6 U.S.C. § 189). Additionally, DHS Directive 143 further directs ONL to serve as the primary point of contact to recommend contracting activity approval for work by the National laboratories, and review all statements of work issued from DHS and directed to the National laboratories.

[14] H.R. Rep. No. 112–492, at 133; S. Rep. No. 112–169, at 15–16.

sibilities for coordinating R&D and coordination processes, as well as a mechanism that tracks all DHS R&D projects, could better position DHS to mitigate the risk of overlapping and unnecessarily duplicative R&D projects. We will continue to monitor DHS's efforts to develop a policy to better coordinate and track R&D activities at the Department.

S&T HAS TAKEN STEPS TO OBTAIN FEEDBACK AND EVALUATE THE IMPACT OF ITS BORDER AND MARITIME R&D EFFORTS

Costs and Types of Completed Border and Maritime R&D Projects Varied

In September 2013, we reported that DHS S&T, Coast Guard, and DNDO reported producing 97 R&D deliverables at an estimated cost of $177 million between fiscal years 2010 and 2012. The type of border and maritime R&D deliverables produced by these R&D entities were wide-ranging in their cost and scale, and included knowledge products and reports, technology prototypes, and software.[15] For example:

- *Knowledge products or reports.*—One of the DHS Centers of Excellence developed formulas and models to assist in randomizing Coast Guard patrol routes and connecting networks together to assist in the detection of small vessels.
- *Technology prototypes.*—S&T BMD developed prototype radar and upgraded video systems for use by Border Patrol Agents and a prototype scanner to screen interior areas of small aircraft without removing panels or the aircraft skin.
- *Software.*—DNDO developed software that extracts data from radiation portal monitors and uses the data to improve algorithms used in detecting radioactive material.

As we reported in September 2013, R&D customers we met with had mixed views on the impact of the R&D deliverables they received. For example, we reviewed the 20 S&T BMD deliverables produced between fiscal years 2010 and 2012 at a cost of $28.7 million. We found that the customers of 7 deliverables stated that the deliverables met their office's needs, customers of 7 did not, customers of 4 did not know, and customers for 2 could not be identified.[16] For example, customers within CBP's Office of Technology Innovation and Acquisition reported that S&T's analysis and test results on aircraft-based use of wide area surveillance technology helped CBP to make a decision on whether it should pursue acquiring such technology. In cases where customers said that the deliverables were not meeting their needs, the customers explained that budget changes, other on-going testing efforts, or changes in mission priorities were the reasons deliverables had not met their needs, and customers pointed out that their relationship with S&T had been positive and highly collaborative. In other cases, customers pointed out that while the deliverable had not been used as intended, it informed their office's decision making and helped to rule out certain technologies as possibilities. In this regard, the customers felt the R&D was successful, despite the fact that the deliverable had not or was not being used.

S&T BMD officials explained that some of its older projects did not have identifiable customers because its former process for selecting projects created the potential to engage in R&D without a clear commitment from the customer. In February 2012, S&T issued a new project management guide that requires project managers to specify the customer by office and name, and to describe customer support for the project, including how the customer has demonstrated commitment for and support of the project. S&T officials said they believed this new process would prevent future R&D funding from going toward projects without a clear customer.

Additionally, we reported that from fiscal year 2010 through fiscal year 2012, DNDO produced 42 deliverables at a cost of $115.9 million, which included 6 discontinued projects and 36 projects that were either transitioned to the next phase of R&D or were completed. DNDO R&D is different from the R&D of S&T for many reasons. For one, a DNDO project may start at a basic research level, and may end up being merged into other similar efforts in order to achieve a higher project goal. In these cases, the R&D customers are DNDO project managers rather than another DHS customer, such as CBP. We discussed 5 DNDO R&D deliverables at various R&D phases with DNDO officials—4 of which were deliverables from on-going or completed projects and 1 of which was a discontinued project. These officials said that the early-stage R&D at DNDO feeds into the prioritized ranking of gaps in the

---

[15] A complete list of all 97 projects for fiscal years 2010 through 2012 and their costs and project type can be found in appendix I of GAO–13–732.

[16] This figure does not include projects from the S&T Office of University Programs, which reported completing 18 border- and maritime-related projects at a cost of $6.1 million.

global nuclear detection architecture, as well as into the analysis-of-alternatives phase of DNDO's solutions development process.[17] Two of the 5 projects we discussed had moved from early-stage R&D into other projects further along in DNDO's project management process. Two of the 5 projects were completed, with 1 project that was reported to have provided information that further informed DNDO decision making and the other project resulting in a commercialized product. With regard to the 1 discontinued project, DNDO officials said that the particular project's technology was determined to be too expensive to continue pursuing.

S&T Did Not Gather and Evaluate Feedback

We reported that although S&T project managers sought feedback from their customers during the execution of projects, S&T did not gather and evaluate feedback from its customers to determine the impact of its completed R&D efforts and deliverables, making it difficult to determine if the R&D met customer needs. Further, in some cases, the customer of S&T's R&D was not clear or the results of the R&D were unknown. For example, a CBP customer identified by S&T was aware of 2 R&D deliverables that S&T said were transitioned to his office, but the official was unable to provide additional information on the project's impact. According to S&T officials, since they deal with multiple DHS components and are not within the same agencies as its customers, it is sometimes difficult to identify who the customer of the R&D is and also difficult to determine what the impact of the R&D was. S&T officials also stated that in S&T's 2012 update to its project management guide, in its project closeout process, S&T has included a step to collect feedback from all relevant customers and a template for collecting this feedback.

While we found in September 2013 that S&T had developed a process and template to collect feedback at the end of each project and incorporated this into its project management plan, we also found that it did not plan to survey customers each time it provides a deliverable to the customer. This is relevant because S&T projects are often conducted over several years before they are concluded and these projects also often produce multiple deliverables for a customer over many years that are designed to meet a specific operational need. For example, the Ground-Based Technologies project began in fiscal year 2006 and is slated to continue through fiscal year 2018. During this period, S&T has provided multiple R&D deliverables to CBP—including test results comparing different ground-based radar systems. The National Academy of Sciences has stated that feedback from both R&D failures and successes may be communicated to stakeholders and used to modify future investments.[18] At the time of our report, S&T had not established time frames and milestones for collecting and evaluating feedback from its customers on the extent to which the deliverables it provides were meeting its customers' needs.

As a result, we recommended that S&T establish time frames and milestones for collecting and evaluating feedback from its customers to determine the usefulness and impact of both its R&D projects and project deliverables, and use it to make better-informed decisions regarding future work. S&T officials concurred with the recommendation at the time of our review, and reported that S&T was developing R&D strategies with DHS components that would include strategic assessments of components' R&D needs and be updated annually on the basis of customer feedback. As of September 2014, S&T has completed strategic plans with Border Patrol, the Transportation Security Administration (TSA), and the Secret Service. Further, at the time of our review, S&T reported that it was developing a new project management guide to improve R&D management at all stages of development, and that the guide would include a template for project managers to use to gather customer feedback on a more consistent basis. In November 2013, S&T finalized its guide, which includes a customer survey template to obtain feedback on the quality and timeliness of a deliverable, as well as detailed descriptions of actions project managers should take throughout the project to ensure the R&D is aligned with customer needs. We will continue to review the implementation of these actions and determine whether they fully address our recommendation to S&T.

DHS Border and Maritime R&D Agencies Have Taken Action to Improve Internal and External R&D Coordination

In September 2013, we also reported that S&T's BMD, the Coast Guard, and DNDO reported taking a range of actions to coordinate with one another and their

[17] The global nuclear detection architecture is an integrated system of radiation detection equipment and interdiction activities to combat nuclear smuggling in foreign countries, at the U.S. border, and inside the United States.
[18] National Academy of Sciences, *Best Practices in Assessment of Research and Development Organizations.* 2012.

customers to ensure that R&D is addressing high-priority needs. Officials from BMD identified several ways in which it coordinates R&D activities with its customers, which are primarily offices within CBP. For example, BMD officials reported having a person detailed to CBP's Office of Technology Innovation and Acquisition and identified its integrated product teams, such as its cross-border tunnel threat team, and jointly-funded projects as ways in which the division works to ensure its R&D efforts are coordinated with CBP. We found that opportunities exist for DHS to enhance coordination with universities conducting R&D on its behalf. Specifically, we reported that the S&T Office of University Programs could help ensure that the approximately $3 million to $4 million a year dedicated to each university center is used more effectively by more carefully considering data needs, potential access issues, and potential data limitations with its Federal partners before approving projects. We recommended that S&T ensure design limitations with regard to data reliability, accessibility, and availability are reviewed and understood before approving Center of Excellence R&D projects. S&T Office of University Programs officials concurred with the recommendation and discussed the variety of ways in which centers and DHS components collaborate and share information. Office of University Programs officials stated that the office's process for soliciting research topics and evaluating proposals is good and that it keeps the centers flexible. However, officials from DHS's primary land border security Center of Excellence reported challenges with respect to a lack of clarity regarding protocols for access to DHS information when conducting R&D. Specifically, officials from this center reported that they have been regularly unable to obtain data from CBP to complete research it was conducting on CBP's behalf, which resulted in delays and terminated R&D projects.

Given the challenges raised by officials from universities leading the R&D for land border security, we recommended that S&T conduct a more rigorous review of potential data-related challenges and limitations at the start of a project in order to help R&D customers (such as CBP) identify data requirements and potential limitations up front so that money is not allocated to projects that potentially cannot be completed. In concurring with our recommendation, S&T Office of University Programs officials agreed that making sure their clients take additional steps to identify data requirements up-front could help address these challenges and following our review had started taking steps to address this. For instance, in September 2013, the Office of University Programs reported that it was working to develop standard guidelines and protocols that would apply to all of its Centers of Excellence. These protocols would describe how data sets must be modified to enable their use in open-source research formats. In March 2014, the Office of University Programs and the National Center for Border Security and Immigration, a DHS S&T Center of Excellence, co-hosted a workshop to identify common problems the centers have in accessing data from DHS, understand DHS constraints in sharing data, and develop best practices for requesting and sharing data between the Centers of Excellence and DHS. We believe this is a step in the right direction and should move S&T closer toward meeting the intention of our recommendation. We will continue to monitor DHS's efforts in this area.

Chairman Meehan, Chairman Buschon, Ranking Member Clarke, Ranking Member Lipinski, and Members of the committees, this completes my prepared statement. I would be happy to respond to any questions you may have at this time.

Mr. MEEHAN. I want to thank the witnesses for their opening statements. I now recognize myself for 5 minutes of questioning.

I appreciate your laying out, in your written testimony, Dr. Brothers, your visionary goals: Screening at speed, trust in cyber future, enable the decision maker and responder of the future. I think those really project some sense in a very difficult environment, where you would like to sort-of see empowerment, but you have just heard the testimony of your oversight partner who is looking at—in the language, you know, fragmented and overlapping activity, working on defining just what research and development is.

But even if it finally gets to a point where people share that definition, you know, how do you track it? So there are some sort of fundamentals that are necessary in order for us to have confidence that the over $1 billion is being—in research funding is being appropriately focused. I applaud you for your vigor with which you have taken on this challenge. Maybe you can share with me your idea of how you take those visions and combine them with the kind of structured plan, so to speak, that will implement more fully the kinds of assurances that there is focus and value associated with the research that is being done.

Under Secretary BROTHERS. I want to thank you for giving me the opportunity to talk about that. So you mentioned the visions. The goal here was to give S&T, our workforce, to give other stakeholders, to give this S&T ecosystem that we talk about—industry, academia, and labs—a common north star, if you will, of where we want to go as an ecosystem. All right, altogether. I think those are 20- or 30-year kind of goals, right? We all understand that.

So now you are getting at, how do we get there? I think that is what—as we mentioned before, the strategy. So now we have got these longer-term visions. Now we have to have to develop a strategy that talks about the baseline of where we are right now with respect to those longer-term visions. It talks where do we want to be in 5 years. It articulates in an actionable way, the ways and means we get there. So that is the next step.

The next step is actually develop this strategy. The framework that we are working on right now, at the end of this year we will be completed of that. Then we should be getting the full document to share. So that is the next step, is getting the strategy going. Now, there are other parts of this that have to work together. So if we look at the strategy, the strategy is gonna have essentially three parts to it. We have to talk about how do we generate capability gaps.

So I want to make a little distinction here between one thing that was mentioned earlier in the opening comments: Our role as providing support for acquisition, which we are doing within the Secretary's Unity of Effort initiatives. Also our responsibility to provide advanced science technology capabilities. To do that, we define capability gaps. So let's think of it this way. This is my favorite teacup. The capability gap that I need to fill for this teacup was how to keep the water for some number of hours, longer than most meetings.

That is a capability gap. Research had to go into materials that would enable us—enable somebody to do that affordably. They had to come up with how heavy this thing should be, what color it should be, all that. That is where we are getting into requirements. So we now have requirements is associated with the acquisition support, capability gaps with our R&D. So that said, we ought to start thinking about, how do we do our capability gap generation?

Here is what I would like to do. I talked to both Dr. O'Toole——

Mr. MEEHAN. Can I ask you—you are talking about capability gaps, and I get that. But one of the pieces that frustrates me, but I think it is understandable, is when any of us contemplate the universe of potential actions that could happen to us it is easy to almost be overwhelmed when you think about the thousands of ways in which we must protect ourselves. I think, in reality, the smart approach is not to worry about every single thing, but to be prioritizing and looking to identify ways in which we can minimize the risks that we are facing and focus, in a way.

How do you take these objectives, which are sort of far-reaching, and put some discipline into the organization so that we don't see what often happens in bureaucracies and other things? People get a vested stake in what they are doing.

Under Secretary BROTHERS. That is absolutely right.

Mr. MEEHAN. They are saying this is important to me. It can be directed by outside influences and get the ear of somebody that says, hey, I got a great new technology, you guys got to be researching this. Things get their own institutional imperative. How do you ride herd over the big mass of movement and give it focus and direction to say, hey, no, these are the priorities and these are the things that we need to focus on to maximize the potential as both to be a shield against potential future harm with changing technologies that we know constantly change the nature of that harm, as well as, you know, the needs that we have to protect ourselves?

Under Secretary BROTHERS. So I think we have to look at analytic capabilities to try to figure that out. Because, like you said, you could have the threat of the day phenomenon. Or you could have some—as you said, someone could have their favorite project. So as you probably know, S&T does threat assessments—threat risk assessments, TRAs, in different areas. There are also a variety of analyses that have looked at what are the probability of various threats versus their impact. So if you look—if you think about this.

So you have got some set of threats, some probability it will happen—whether it is not that likely versus very likely. Then on the other axis, you might have high-impact. What we should be looking at, I believe, are those things that are high-impact. We can't just look at things that are low-probability, high-impact because other things will happen. So I think we first start with that. What are the things that are high-impact, potentially high-impact? There is analysis that look at that, right, both from the public—from the private sector as well as from the Federal Government.

So we start winnowing down our portfolio based on those. Now, internally, you see the apex. So internally we have got these visions. What we have done, then, is talk to our component partners to try to come up with, so what are the things we should really focus on? When I first came to this position, I asked the folks in directorate to give me a review of the different projects, to understand really what we are doing, what our investments are going towards.

We did that. It is a very good process. It is a very good process, it helped in a number of ways. It helped for everyone in the organization to understand what we are doing. But in doing so, I understood that we have a lot of projects that some of which are of lower investment value or potentially lower-impact. So my goal is, then, to consolidate some of those programs so we have higher impact in specifically-targeted areas. So those are the areas that we are calling these Apex programs.

So Dr. O'Toole, the prior Secretary, had Apex programs that were primarily 2-year in extent, in time duration. I would like to extend those to 5 years. But I would like to have those—have more of them so that we can have real impact in the areas that are high-impact in terms of threat, that we have buy-in from operational partners. But not only that, that are in the art of the possible, scientifically and technically, to come up with a solution.

Mr. MEEHAN. So let me—already, thank you for that. I want to be careful that I don't run over too significantly on my time. I know you can develop that further in questions that will be generated by my colleagues.

So in that line, allow me to recognize the gentleman from New Jersey, Mr. Payne, for any questions he may have.

Mr. PAYNE. Thank you, Mr. Chairman. Under Secretary, it is really good to have you here, and congratulations for coming through the confirmation process unscathed, maybe.

Under Secretary BROTHERS. I didn't say that.

Mr. PAYNE. Possibly. You know, over the years this subcommittee has seen a number of direct reports to the under secretary vary. There are benefits and costs of streamlining the organizational structure to reduce the number of direct reports to the under secretary. Have you had a chance to evaluate the number of direct reports to you? If so, are you planning any changes?

Under Secretary BROTHERS. So when I came into the organization I was aware of kind of three guiding principles for thinking about reorganization. The first one is form follows function. Form follows function. So what I want to do is, once we developed our strategy is then try to understand what that implies with the organization. I don't want to come in without that and start reorganizing for the sake of doing so. So form follows function. We will have a strategy, we will reorganize to effectively carry out that strategy.

The second principle is maximizing efficiencies, obviously. So that is what we will have to look at, and we are doing some of that right now within existing structures. The third part is, reorganization leads to disruption. So my third guiding principle is, minimize disruption. We have got some—not a lot of time to deal with some very important threats. The more we disrupt our workforce, the less efficiently and effectively we will be able to carry out our mission. So my goal is to minimize the disruption in working day-to-day of our workforce, while simultaneously have an organization where form truly follows function and we can most effectively achieve the strategy that we will be building and sharing with you in the near future.

Mr. PAYNE. But you—do you see a need for streamlining in terms of the number of reports that——

Under Secretary BROTHERS. I can't say I see a need right now.

Mr. PAYNE. Okay.

Under Secretary BROTHERS. I can say that as we are looking for the strategy I will have more information, going forward. But I don't look for—I do not look for major reorganization.

Mr. PAYNE. Okay, in the area of basic research and innovation——

Under Secretary BROTHERS. Yes.

Mr. PAYNE [continuing]. Could you give us an update on the overview of the agreement between S&T Advanced Research Projects Agency and TSA entitled "Research and development tests and evaluation strategic plan" that was signed in 2013?

Under Secretary BROTHERS. So I can give you some sense of that. For more detail, I will be more than glad to get back with you on that. I actually met with the TSA CTO recently to talk about our relationship. We have simultaneously worked on strategies. So where we are—right now, S&T is working on road maps, our technology road maps. These are influencing and have been influenced by what our component partners do. For example, the strategy at the TSA, the agreement that you mentioned.

We are currently working with TSA on—in fundamental areas—including explosives detection. In more applied areas, including actually developing devices. In the deployment phase, as well. So we are looking—working with TSA across the full life cycle, trying to understand how we can most quickly and also effectively get new technologies out there to combat newer threats.

Mr. PAYNE. Okay. You know, along those lines, you know the committee has always asked that S&T develop and implement clear and transparent processes and criteria for identifying basic research and innovation, needs, prioritizing projects, and selecting performers. However, it is always an issue of contention that there is no clear basis for concluding that the current allocation of basic research is appropriate S&T-wide among the components or within the individual components.

What will be your plan and process in selecting basic and innovation research projects? Will there be a transparent process by which to prioritize basic research across components and within the components?

Under Secretary BROTHERS. Yes. So—let me talk about some mechanisms that exist now, and how I think we can scale across the enterprise. So every year, S&T does a portfolio review. We call this our "navigant" review. In this review, we have a panel of experts, including S&T and from outside stakeholders, and we brief our programs to this panel. During this process, the panel weighs these projects according to a variety of parameters, including customer buy-in, technical feasibility, novel approach—these kind of metrics, or axes if you want to put it on a graph, okay?

At the end of that, one of what I think significant scales they come up with is one that plots feasibility versus impact. Over the past few years, we have used this—or it has been used by—in previous—by the previous under secretary to figure out where, on this plot—you think about it, feasibility and horizontal axis impact on a vertical axis where the project should fall. How they should map. So if you think about the upper right part of that, what you find is that is gonna be the high-impact, high-feasibility projects. So it is more near-term.

That is where the projects have been focused recently. Listening to some of the opening statements here and my own belief of having a more balanced portfolio, I think it is important, as we go through that analytic process—that navigant, that portfolio review process—I think it is important to think about these other quadrants of that graph I was mentioning to have our product—our investments. So in answer to your question, I think it is important we go through this analytic process and look across those areas.

Now, the Coast Guard is also using the same process. So this process can be scaled to beyond just S&T. This is something we can then use. The results of that process are then something that we can use as a way of not just understanding where our portfolio is, but trying to influence where the portfolio should go in the future.

Now, there is another piece I want to mention, as well. We started this with Chairman Meehan's comments, my comments with Chairman Meehan. This has to do with how we are generating the capability gaps.

What I would like to see is, where we actually have a model based on what I have seen in the industry. Where you have a central research facility, where you have a common—where you have a centralized resources of staff, of infrastructure, et cetera. Then these larger corporations also have research capabilities in the business areas. Or in our case, these would be our end-users, our components. So this could be DNDO, it could be Coast Guard. Now, what we do that—what the laboratories in industry that have been successful, what they do is they embed their staff into their business units.

That gives their technical staff members the opportunity to understand the context in which they work. So it is not just designing something that an engineer thinks is useful. It is designing something that the actual end-user, the Customs Border Patrol Agent, thinks is useful. So that, and then we will have liaisons from the components to come back. We hope to actually pilot that starting in November.

Mr. PAYNE. Okay. Thank you, Mr. Chairman. I am well over my time.

So I will yield back.

Mr. MEEHAN. Well, I thank the gentleman. If there is an important question that you want to either have one of our colleagues ask, or if we need to return to an issue that needs to be clarified, we will certainly work with that.

At this point in time, let me turn it to my good friend and colleague, the gentleman from Indiana, Mr. Bucshon.

Mr. BUCSHON. Thank you, Mr. Chairman. Since my time—I have been here in Congress now almost 4 years, and I have been surprised—somewhat surprised about how a lot of GAO reports seem to be minimized by everyone, honestly. I have been a little concerned recently, where some in the administration have been overtly critical of the role the GAO serves on behalf of the American people. I would suggest that a fair critique of GAO reports is expected, however overt suggestions of political motivation should be avoided by all.

With that said, Dr. Brothers, the GAO reported that the S&T does not know its total investment in R&D, and described the difficulty you have had in conducting basic Government audits for how taxpayer funds are being spent. The GAO's initial audit was completed 2 years ago. While DHS agreed with the findings and recommendations, it doesn't seem much has been done to fix the problem. This is where I am getting at not necessarily being minimized or ignored, but it just seems like GAO reports come and go and we don't do anything.

So why is it so difficult to answer the simple question of how much is being spent on R&D? What efforts does S&T have under way to reliably track costs associated with R&D activities?

Under Secretary BROTHERS. So in the beginning, I think this came out of the GAO report, was the first recommendation was defining R&D. So the first part of the problem has happened in the past. You know, in July we did release new—a definition of R&D. But in the past, we didn't have that definition. So that means different people that have different definitions of what research and development really is.

Mr. BUCSHON. Can I interrupt for a second?

Under Secretary BROTHERS. Absolutely.

Mr. BUCSHON. It is amazing to me that after decades and decades of the Government looking at these things that the fundamental definition of what constitutes R&D is something that we don't have.

Under Secretary BROTHERS. I understand. We do——

Mr. BUCSHON. I am not blaming you. I am just—that is just an editorial comment.

Under Secretary BROTHERS. So I think, you know, based on OMB, based on DOD definitions, NASA definitions, as well, we have crafted our own definition of what R&D is. So we have used the same type of nomenclature—basic applied development—is then banded into different areas—6–1, 6–2, 6–3, et cetera, which allow us—which will allow us, going forward, to do a better job of understanding, from a data call perspective, who is doing what in R&D and where it lies.

Can I bring up another piece, too? That is a——

Mr. BUCSHON. I will have one more question after you finish your answer to this.

Under Secretary BROTHERS. Okay.

Mr. BUCSHON. So if you could give me the time to do that.

Under Secretary BROTHERS. Speed it up? Okay. I would like to address this issue of overlap a little bit. Because when I was in DOD we sponsored a study. The study was looking at the DOD laboratories. It was looking at the DOD laboratories to see what kind of overlap there might be, whether innovative with respect to private industry, those kinds of things. It was also really interesting. Because what they showed was that there was this taxonomy of R&D, at one level.

So maybe the level is—and I will make this quick—was wireless communications. Maybe found that a lot of the laboratories are doing wireless communications. But when the study was complete, and then you could say at that level there was a lot of overlap. What the study found, interesting enough, was when you broke it down to a high-enough level of fidelity they, indeed, weren't overlapped. There wasn't overlap. Because one lab might be doing a lot of work in protocols, one work might be doing a lot of work in, actually, the radio design itself.

So part of the problem we have is the definition of R&D itself. But also the taxonomy that we are using to describe what the particular project is. So that becomes another problem, as well, and you have to break it down into higher fidelity. So I just want to say that.

Mr. BUCSHON. Sure. I mean, I think you have a unique opportunity, coming from DOD and now you are at DHS, to really try to help coordinate these two agencies. Along that lines, I am interested in what you might be able to do. For example, there are mobile surveillance assets that DOD uses in Afghanistan and other places that also may have a significant role in protecting our borders, for example. We don't want to reinvent the wheel here.

There are a lot of things that are currently at DOD that probably can be used to protect us here in the homeland. Whether it is at our borders or other—or internal surveillance within our own country, where it is appropriate, to make sure that we don't—aren't attacked. Can you just comment on what you think you can do, having experience at both these agencies, and how you can help coordinate that? Maybe look at how we can use DOD assets for homeland security.

Under Secretary BROTHERS. Yes, I appreciate that question. I have thought about this. I think right now there are mechanisms to allow us to do this. We have the capabilities development working group, which is DOD and DHS getting together to talk about potentially joint efforts, what we might be able to use from DOD. We also have something called the Mission Executive Council. That is made up of members of DHS, DOE, Office of Director of National Intelligence and—yes, I think that is about it. So we have got— and, plus, we have got the Committee on Homeland National Security, which is chaired by the White House, myself, and ASDRNE, which is essentially CTO of Department of Defense.

So we have these mechanisms. I think—well, I talked about my priorities coming into the position—you know, the visions of strategy, that type of thing. My priorities going forward, starting out, are implementation. That is the first one. I think in order to implement the kind of programs we are talking about, these Apex programs, we have to do a good job of leveraging what our agency partners possess, as well. I think that is what you are getting at. I think we do have the mechanism to do that, but I think we have to do a better job. That is what I plan to do is align this.

So if we have some number of Apex projects, some number of farside that we are concentrating on, that has to be communicated to these interagency groups. We have to pull folks together to work on these important projects. So we actually have a critical mass.

Mr. BUCSHON. Yes, I think if we can get back—past the proprietary nature that some different agencies have, and also turf—you know, protecting your turf.

Under Secretary BROTHERS. Yes, yes.

Mr. BUCSHON. You can really—you are in a unique position, being both—at both places to really make a difference.

I yield back, Mr. Chairman.

Mr. MEEHAN. I thank the gentleman.

Now I recognize Mr. Lipinski, from Illinois.

Mr. LIPINSKI. Thank you, Mr. Chairman. Over the past few years, DHS has eliminated much of the basic research in order to produce more deliverables. I am wondering, and this is sort-of following up from what Mr. Payne was saying, Under Secretary Brothers, do you think that more work needs to be done on basic research? Where do you see the importance of basic research for the S&T Directorate at Homeland Security? Or do you see that this basic research should be coming from elsewhere? I just was wondering how important you think basic research is to—directly to your mission.

I know it is—we all know it is important, but how much has to be done, the basic research needs to be done, by you under the S&T Directorate?

Under Secretary BROTHERS. So I think basic research is important. I think that we have a unique opportunity because we have nine Centers of Excellence. These Centers of Excellence are university-based, they have university researchers that can be focused on our priorities. Specific examples of where basic research is important is phenomenological research. So if we are starting to look at homemade explosives, and we need to understand what are different detection modalities and methodologies, that is where basic research can come in.

So it is important that we engage our university partners, our Centers of Excellence, as well as outside universities in this kind of research, but with the context of where we are going. I think what I have seen in past roles has been that university research sometimes can lead to a paper, a publication. What we need is, we are to lead to a capability. But if we give them the—if we give a universe research—and we are actually doing this with our Office of University Programs right now. Where our Centers of Excellence are aligned with our goals.

So I think, to answer your question, it is important. I think we do—we are doing it already right now. My second priority—so my first priority, going forward, is implementation. My second priority is alignment. That is part of the alignment priority right there is getting our universities more fundamentally aligned with where S&T is trying to go.

Mr. LIPINSKI. Do you see any changes needed in the university centers, or just in general with the process that—the whole process of having the centers? Do you think this is working well? I am not offering—I am not saying that it is not. I just want to know what your thoughts were on it.

Under Secretary BROTHERS. Yes, yes. So, you know, it is interesting. During my confirmation hearing I had a number of briefings on that. I was immediately impressed with the competence of our Office of University Programs. I was impressed because I found that while it can be very difficult sometimes for a Government agency to work with a university because of the difference in time lines, because of the way they have structured the program, our Office of University Programs that is, I think we effectively and efficiently used these universities to get some good capabilities.

Mr. LIPINSKI. Now, what about the—doing more to utilize the DOE National labs. Do you think—do you believe DHS takes adequate advantage of access to the DOE labs?

Under Secretary BROTHERS. I think we take adequate advantage of access to DOE labs, which is in our authorization language. I think, again, with alignment we could do a better job with alignment. That is something I plan to do. But I think there is a lot of exchange with the DOE laboratories and that should continue. The DOE labs have unique capabilities that the homeland security enterprise needs. I think we have to continue to take advantage of that.

Mr. LIPINSKI. Do you see any obstacles that we could work on eliminating? Are there any obstacles through your work with the DOE labs?

Under Secretary BROTHERS. I don't know of any particular obstacles right now, but I appreciate the question.

Mr. LIPINSKI. Okay. Well, as we move forward here, and I know there is a lot of work that needs to be done, the question, obviously, that continues to come up and has been talked about—you talked about it and you have answered a little bit in the questions—is the—determining and really getting a handle on, as the GAO said, a handle on the money that is spent on research by—in the S&T Directorates. I just want to say that I think it is important that we continue to work together on that, to do that. It is really critical that we do take advantage of the great resources we have in this country at universities and also at the DOE labs to help to do this research, both basic and applied research.

So look forward to working with you on that, and I will yield back the balance of my time.

Under Secretary BROTHERS. Thank you.

Mr. MEEHAN. I thank the gentleman.

Now recognize the gentleman from Ohio, Mr. Johnson.

Mr. JOHNSON. Thank you, Mr. Chairman. Gentlemen, thank you for joining us today.

Dr. Brothers, given DHS S&T's relatively small budget and the problems GAO has found to date, how confident are you that DHS is producing the technologies that are most needed for homeland security?

Under Secretary BROTHERS. I think we have the capability to do that. I think that some of the processes that were talked a little bit about this morning. The portfolio review, where we can actually get strategic alignment across not just S&T, but also the enterprise. I think we can do that. I think by having a—the Unity of Effort the Secretary is championing. I think that we can have much more effective and efficient acquisition programs. I think by having the types of relationships with the components we can generate solid capability gaps from which to derive our research investment portfolio. So I think we can do this. I think we have a capability, I think we have the workforce that can do this.

Mr. JOHNSON. Okay, all right. Well, how do the—for both of you—how do the DHS components in S&T determine which of their technology needs can be bought off the shelf, and which require research and development? What is the process by which common needs across the components are evaluated, prioritized, and then passed to S&T for implementation? You can decide who goes first.

Mr. MAURER. Thanks for the question. That is an issue that DHS has historically struggled with. Trying to determine the common needs of the Department, working across components, coming up with common requirements. We are encouraged by the fact that the Secretary has this new focus on Unity of Effort and is implementing different approaches to translating the strategic priorities of the Department into acquisition requirements as well as, hopefully, drive what R&D is going to do to fill capabilities gaps. We have had a high-risk area for a number of years for DHS management and this has been one of the areas where, frankly, DHS still has some ways to go, translating what they want to do into actual programs that meet cost and schedule milestones.

Mr. JOHNSON. Okay.

Under Secretary BROTHERS. So I think that we have something we call technology-foraging, where we have our staff members, our stakeholders understand what is out there in the world, so to speak. So, for example, our first responders group, they have an effort where they meet with first responders directly. They in a sense have a forum, where they meet with first responders and understand what their priorities are. I have a list right here of their priorities, of what they are. They go from situational awareness, safety, protection, these kinds of things.

So I think that is a great example of how one of the organizations within S&T actually directly captures needs from the actual end-users and can translate those into programs. I think those are the kinds of ideas that have to be scaled across S&T as well as the Department, as well. So I think that is a case study of how it can work.

Mr. JOHNSON. Well, speaking of the first responders, I assume that you are taking a lot of input from first responders to find out what they think they need to respond to the different types of threats and situations that they face. Is that——

Under Secretary BROTHERS. That is absolutely correct. That is part of that forum that I was mentioned a few minutes ago. Where we get tremendous input from across the country from first responders. We bring them in to talk to us about what their needs are, and then we develop a prioritized list of what they say they need. So I think it is very effective. In fact, that is then being used to influence our first responder of the future Apex program. Where we are looking at, how can we use the current technology and emerging technology in wearables, ruggedize it, and really apply it to the first responder mission sets?

Mr. JOHNSON. Okay. Well, Mr. Maurer, and you might have alluded to this. But I was wondering if you could expand on any recommendations that you might make to ensure that technology needs are properly vetted before S&T develops an R&D program to support it.

Mr. MAURER. Yes, absolutely. I think we would really underscore a couple of things. One is it is important that they are developing a new strategy, a new strategic approach, going forward. Because I think it is time to update that. The last one was done in 2011. There has been a new Quadrennial Homeland Security Review to drive strategic priorities. We want to see that translated into how S&T does its line of business. So strategy is important.

Tightening the coordination links between S&T and the operational components is absolutely critical. Whatever S&T works on, it is not going to be used in the real world unless there is that hand-off to the components. There are a lot of different forums that they are developing to enhance that and improve that. The closer they can work with eventual end-users the better off they are going to be.

Mr. JOHNSON. Okay. Well, I thank you for your responses.

Mr. Chairman, I yield back.

Mr. MEEHAN. I thank the gentleman.

The Chairman now recognizes the Ranking Member of the full Committee on Homeland Security.

Mr. THOMPSON. Thank you, Mr. Chairman. Taking off from Mr. Payne and Mr. Johnson's comments, Dr. Brothers, it would be an understatement to say that the relationship with components and S&T has been anything but cordial. So how do you plan, in your new role at S&T, to bridge what some see as your lack of respect for S&T or just total disregard for the work you do? Take TSA, for example.

Under Secretary BROTHERS. So, yes, glad you mentioned that. Because we are meeting regularly with TSA, both Administrator Pistole and with CTO, to discuss what their needs are. I really can report to you today that we are working hand-in-hand with TSA, reporting up into headquarters on our work addressing some emerging threats. So I think a lot of this has to do with relationship building. In the 4 months I have been there I have met with all the component heads, some of them more than one time, to try to develop that kind of relationship. Really, a lot of it is listening.

I mean, part of science and technology is that you have smart engineers—and I saw this in industry—can come up with an idea. But because they don't have the context for their work, they don't have the relationship with the end-user, it is not relevant. It is just not relevant. It is an interesting thing, but it is not relevant. So our job, then, is to reach out and help them understand what the art of the possible is and we understand what their needs are, both near-term and long-term. I think we have started that. I think TSA is a great example. Because we really are working hand-in-hand with TSA right now.

Mr. THOMPSON. So, Mr. Maurer, is this part of that hand-off you were referring to in your earlier comments?

Mr. MAURER. Yes, absolutely. There needs to be the bridge between ideas and technology and approaches that are being researched within S&T and the operational components. You have scientists and engineers who are coming up with good ideas, developing new technologies, new softwares. That is all fine and good. But eventually, at some point, the hope is it is gonna be used in the real world to help secure the borders or secure the homeland, execute DHS' missions. For that to happen we have to have that bridge between S&T and the components.

That is gonna take—that is, frankly, gonna take some time to work on. It is gonna include the high-level discussions that the under secretary talked about. It is gonna include staff-level discussions so that the folks down in the trenches know what each other is—know what each other is working on. Even S&T there is gonna be a renewed focus and a renewed emphasis on filling capabilities gaps, developing bridges between filling those gaps and supporting major acquisition programs.

Mr. THOMPSON. Let me add another component to that. If the process is cumbersome, then you really only get big players in the marketplace. Small, medium-sized businesses don't have the capacity in terms of resources to stay in the marketplace in the R&D mode rather than operational. How do you plan, Mr. Brothers, to close that gap so small business can compete with new ideas just like big businesses?

Under Secretary BROTHERS. So it is my belief that small—that a lot of some of the most innovative and creative solutions can come from small business. I believe that. I have seen that happen. However, some of the small businesses aren't familiar with the way that the Federal Government does business. I think it is important that we reach out in different ways, not just the standard ways that we do things. One way to do this is through reaching out via social media. I think an example of that where we have seen tremendous response has been just sending out these visionary goals for comment and review.

In the week we have had it, we have had about 1,500 people sign up for the website. We have had comments that aren't just about the visionary goals. They are comments about science and technology across different capabilities that the community thinks we should think about. What this has let me know is that there is a conversation, a National conversation, about S&T and Homeland Security that needs to take place. So we plan to follow up on that.

So let me get back directly to your question. Those are the types—that is the type of media outreach that we—that can engage the small business community. I think that is what we plan to keep doing. Now, the next question is, well, how do we get to them? So that is where you can talk about our other transactions authority. So right now, we have another transaction authority that is appropriated every year. What would be helpful is to have that permanent with us. But it is those kinds of—so it is that kind of outreach, as well as the mechanisms for working with small businesses, that can be very helpful. That is what I hope to push forward on.

Mr. THOMPSON. Well—and I think, Dr. Brothers, if you can get it out of the social media context and get it into an operational context. Those small businesses say we get invited to sessions all the time, but we can't translate the fluff of people saying we are open for business from reality. The reality is do I really have a chance to show my bright ideas, or is this just another check-the-box kind-of event? I think—and I don't really look for an answer, but I want you to think about, as you try to broaden that participation that there are really some actionable things at the end of it rather than just 1,500 social media contacts.

Under Secretary BROTHERS. I appreciate that feedback. I think one of the things—I am gonna take a second to comment. I appreciate the feedback a lot because I am trying to understand ways to do better outreach to that community. I think we have been thinking about having industry days. The Department of Defense has days where they actually try to do match—matchmaking between smaller businesses and larger businesses. That may be a model. But I do appreciate the feedback because I think we need to think hard about how to not just get folks interested in what we are doing, but engage them in a meaningful way, like you are getting at.

Mr. THOMPSON. Thank you very much. If you want to pursue it at some point, I would love to continue the discussion.

Under Secretary BROTHERS. Thank you, appreciate it.

Mr. THOMPSON. I yield back, Mr. Chairman.

Mr. MEEHAN. Thank you, Chairman.

The Chairman now recognizes Mr. Collins for his questioning.

Mr. COLLINS. Thank you, Mr. Chairman. Dr. Brothers, I am just curious. I mean, a lot of us were worried about every dollar we spend, and if there is overlap that is probably, there is some level of waste. So to me, an example is always one of the best places to try to figure out what is going on. If you look at DARPA and maybe in the bioterrorism world, and then you look at DHS and your operation—and even pick one thing like anthrax that has been going on now almost 15 years—how does the department—DHS and your department overlap with DARPA on something like a bioterrorism threat like anthrax? Is—should there be two departments involved in something like that?

Under Secretary BROTHERS. I think you—it would—the answer depends. It depends on specifically what they are doing. I think that goes back to what I was mentioning earlier about the study that we had at DOD that looked at how different laboratories were doing things that seemed like they were the same. When you reach down in higher fidelity and actually look at it, it is not the same. So one of the things that you can think about is there may be different ways of solving the same problem. Some may be shorter-term, some may be more effective than others, some may be the 80 percent solution, some may be going for the 100 percent solution.

So when you start looking at a different—an effort, for example, in bioterrorism, you have to look very carefully along all these different dimensions of the effort. So I think there is space for different agencies to work in that domain. I think it is important that there is some—there is visibility between the agencies, and we—and DARPA, specifically, we do have that kind of visibility. But I think that it is important, and I think there is a space for different agencies in those kind of areas.

Mr. COLLINS. So you wouldn't think if one agency, DOD, had responsibility for something like bioterrorism, I would assume that they would pursue all these different avenues. They don't need another agency maybe duplicating people thinking through the same problem. I think, in the private sector, we would never have a case where you knowingly had two departments working on the same thing and think that is a good thing.

Under Secretary BROTHERS. If we take another example, take cyber. So we consider cyber, where as it is defined the DOD and DHS have somewhat different areas. We are still doing research in cyber and we are still collaborating in cyber. But our spaces are, while overlapping—they are overlapping—while overlapping, they are distinct in some ways. So it is important to understand that and to work in those spaces like that.

Mr. COLLINS. So let's go back at anthrax for a second. So after 15 years what would—do you think this country is ready if there was an anthrax attack tomorrow?

Under Secretary BROTHERS. I guess I would have to say it depends on the scope. I would also have to say that to get into more details about this I would like to follow up with you in that specific threat area to have a more detailed conversation.

Mr. COLLINS. Well, if you were talking about scope. Somebody weaponizes anthrax, puts it into an air conditioning system, blows it into a shopping mall. So there is no thought that anyone is exposed. So not unlike the post office, where you could use Cipro as a prophylactic to treat it before it became symptomatic. But—so now you got a shopping center. It blew through there, no one had any idea, now they are post-symptomatic. I mean, best I know it is still 95 percent death.

Under Secretary BROTHERS. Like I said, I would like to come back to you on that discussion. Appreciate that.

Mr. COLLINS. I would——

Under Secretary BROTHERS. Okay.

Mr. COLLINS [continuing]. As well. including some other things, like Ebola now, the bird flu, SARS. I am—I think in the bioterrorism area, DARPA is very, very involved. I wasn't, until I read this, didn't even realize that the Department of Homeland Security had involvement in that.

Under Secretary BROTHERS. Yes.

Mr. COLLINS. Yes, I would like to follow up.

Under Secretary BROTHERS. Please. Thank you. Appreciate that.

Mr. MEEHAN. I am assuming you yield back. I don't want to jump into your space, Mr. Collins, but I thank you for your questioning.

The Chairman now recognizes Ms. Kelly from Illinois. Thank you, Ms. Kelly.

Ms. KELLY. Thank you, Mr. Chairman. Good morning.

Under Secretary BROTHERS. Good morning.

Ms. KELLY. We have seen, in multiple GAO reports—and have heard from security and technical experts as well as other outside stakeholders that DHS lacks a strategic plan for the agency's research investments. This has been going on for some time. So we have listened to a lot of things that you said you are doing or want to do. What is your biggest sign that you are on the right track? Also what are obstacles that you are concerned about? Both of you can answer that.

Under Secretary BROTHERS. Sure. I think the signs I am on the right track, the enthusiasm of the workforce, the enthusiasm of components—so—I have got a lot of response on the visionary goals in the components. I have got a lot of interest in the components on having this embedding program. You know, what I am interested in doing is having kind of a virtual IPT. I think in the past, in terms of generating capability gaps, there have been IPTs that have been formed. I would like to do an embedded IPT, if you will. There has been a lot of enthusiasm for that.

I have regular meetings with headquarters, with the deputy secretary, with the component heads. I think we are getting—we are involved with the Senior Leadership Council. So with the Secretary's Unity of Effort, he has put together some structure. The Senior Leadership Council, a deputies management advisory group, and a joint requirements council. We have a seat on all of those. So I think because of this Unity of Effort initiative of the Secretary's, and because of relationships we are building, I think we can—I think we will be successful.

Mr. MAURER. Yes. I think in terms of positive notes on the progress that the S&T is making, I think the fact that the Department now has a definition for R&D is a good first step. It shows they are being responsive to some of the recommendations from our prior reports. The development of a new strategy is also a positive step. The Secretary's approach for a Unity of Effort which tries to align strategic priorities down through the organization and tighten the linkage between the components and the various operational units in the DHS, those are all positive things.

In terms of challenges, there are a number of challenges. I think first and foremost is the fact that I think what has developed over the course of a number of years is that the components don't necessarily think of S&T as their first-stop shopping center for meeting their needs, their mission needs. That is a challenge that is gonna have to be overcome. I think the morale challenge within S&T is a significant one. You know, 299 out of 300 is not good. That is something that is gonna have to be addressed as part of the overall effort to develop a new strategic approach.

I think the other challenge is the fact that the S&T Directorate is being pulled in a number of different directions. They have a number of different initiatives, a number of different priorities. Trying to address a number of different threats with resources that are a little over a billion dollars a year. A much smaller subset of that is actually discretionary in the sense that they have a lot of flexibility in where it goes. So trying to figure out the areas where they can add the most value, while staying within the confines of constrained budget realities is also gonna be a major challenge going forward.

Ms. KELLY. Any comment on——

Under Secretary BROTHERS. I can comment on that because—I am glad you mentioned the workforce. Because that is—I was—I should mention that. What I have been doing recently has been simple steps. I have been walking around a lot and talking to people. We are gonna do a formal root cause analysis. We should hopefully have that on contract shortly to get that done. But I think in the interim, walking around talking to people, understanding what some of the concerns have been in the past, has been helpful. We have been trying to do more of empowering our workforce in the decision-making process.

Given—giving more visibility in how decisions are made and why decisions are made. I think all that is important. But I do have to agree. That is a challenge. I think it is something that we are very concerned about and putting some—a lot of time into going forward. The other issue of the—you know, many different projects going different ways. We are trying to address that with this consolidation I mentioned earlier in the Apex projects, and trying to have more focus. Again, that is a priority going forward is—the second priority is alignment.

You know, aligning—you know, this—you know, it is about aligning not just our HSARPA investment programs, not just the first responders group investment programs. But it is also the work we do in our small business innovator research program. It is aligning what we are doing in our Centers of Excellence. So it is all of this. It is our—alignment we do in our laboratories. It is aligning what we do in our investments with the Department of Energy laboratories that we were talking about earlier.

So I think that that is all gonna be challenged. It is all about the people. It is aligning people in your goals—in your end goals.

That, by itself, is a large challenge. But that is what we have to do if we are gonna get the most out of S&T in our investments.

Ms. KELLY. Thank you.

Under Secretary BROTHERS. Thank you.

Ms. KELLY. I yield back.

Mr. MEEHAN. Thank you. Thanks, Ms. Kelly.

The Chairman now recognizes Mr. Hultgren from Illinois. I knew that.

Mr. HULTGREN. Thanks, Mr. Chairman. Thank you, Mr. Chairman. Really appreciate the witnesses for being here. This is an important, timely discussion to be having so I really do appreciate it. I think this is important for us to be having this joint hearing today. So thank you so much for being here.

Border security certainly is becoming an increasingly difficult problem to deal with. I believe our ability to deploy better technologies to that effort works as, really, a force multiplier that keeps not only our Nation, but also our boots on the ground, more safe. It has been good to receive your testimony as we continue to ensure that taxpayer dollars are spent wisely with a clear strategy and set goal that must be accomplished.

Dr. Brothers, I wanted to address my first question to you. How does DHS define success for research and development programs?

Under Secretary BROTHERS. So, first I want—let me make a comment. That one of the things I want to institute more of is fast failure. So I think one thing we have to understand as we talk about having a balanced portfolio that goes from, you know, low risk to higher right, with larger potential impact is, there has to be acknowledgment that there will be failure. So—however, the way to manage that is to fail quickly. So that means, in the conversations earlier were about metrics, that means having appropriate metrics for these programs so you can determine when these programs should fail.

Now, in terms of success it depends on where you are in that research spectrum. Because if you are doing basic research you are probably not gonna say success is transitioning that basic research directly to the component. But I think if you look across the breadth of our research responsibilities, which go from basic research all the way up to acquisition support, I think success is that. It is transitioning a meaningful capability to our end-users.

Mr. HULTGREN. Really, following up on that and, again, Dr. Brothers and also Mr. Maurer, what is the current system of transfer technology from the research and development stage to implementation? I wondered how long it typically takes to deploy a new technology? Dr. Brothers, I will start with you and then Mr. Maurer.

Under Secretary BROTHERS. Yes, sure. So that is another "it depends." Because some of technologies—for example first responder technologies—which the first responder group which works more near-term, more integrating existing commercial technologies, that is gonna be shorter-term. That might be in a period of 18 months or so, something like that. However, some of the more fundamentally research-based efforts, like these maybe H, homemade, explosives detection—where you are actually going from new modalities to actual equipment to actual deployment in an airport—that could take years.

Because that—because part of the transition isn't just understanding, does the science indeed work? It is not just have I produced a prototype that can be tested effectively. It is also by going through all the qualification/certification testing and all that, as well as training of the end-users. So while the front-end research can take some number of years, it can take a significant amount of time to do qualification testing and training, as well. So that can be years.

Mr. HULTGREN. Mr. Maurer, any thoughts?

Mr. MAURER. Yes, absolutely. It is not a quick process to translate ideas into real-life devices that are in the hands of end-users. I agree with everything that Dr. Brothers mentioned. I want to emphasize in particular, when you are thinking about real-world deployment it is not just the technology itself. It is also the training, it is the support, it is the maintenance. There are a lot of things that are involved in turning an idea into something that is being used to secure the homeland.

Mr. HULTGREN. I understand it is not an easy process, but it also is an important process. You have to make sure that if there are bureaucratic hurdles that are slowing down the process to getting something that literally could save lives, we have got to make sure that that gets done and we address those things, as well. Certainly, we want to do it the right way.

Under Secretary BROTHERS. Sure.

Mr. HULTGREN. But I also get frustrated when things take longer than they should. That is our goal, that is our hope. Dr. Brothers, in years past concerns were expressed that sometimes the Department allows for security needs to be defined by end-users who do not necessarily incorporate technical or economic feasibility. How can you ensure that the research enterprise is somewhat insulated from predetermined outcomes allowing for the department—development, excuse me, of transformational technologies that we can't even envision today? That respond to threats that we aren't aware of today? How can we get innovative solutions instead of just the next gadget?

Under Secretary BROTHERS. So I think the reason why I started out with my discussion of requirements versus capability gaps, I think is my emphasis to make sure we have the right lexicon for talking about it. Because I think we—because of the Unity of Effort initiative, which has the Joint Requirements Council on it, which were the principles from the components and headquarters components—including S&T, MMPD, et cetera—sit on, that is where the acquisition decisions are made. So that actually has a component in it for developing requirements—we sit on that board—for doing system analysis. We provide staff for that, as well.

So from the acquisition perspective, the way the Secretary has structured the organization now, with this Joint Requirements Council, we are right there at the table to work with the components in defining requirements and defining the systems engineering piece of the acquisition process. As well as doing the operational test evaluation. Along with that, it turns out that a lot of the tests in programs is in the early parts of it. That is something we might want to get involved in, as well. Currently, we are not as involved. We might want to get involved in that, as well.

Now let's go to the other part of the question. That is the disruptive technologies, the capabilities that you were talking about a moment ago. That is back to capabilities part and capability gaps part. I think, with this embedded IPT that I was talking about earlier, that will help us get to those needs that aren't colored by, hey, I just want, you know, the next thing like this. So I think by having the right lexicon by talking about requirements and capability gaps, having a willingness to accept risk from high—from potentially disruptive programs, I think we can make the difference known.

Mr. HULTGREN. Thank you. I want to thank my Chairman and my other Chairman. Larry, thank you.

Appreciate this.

Mr. MEEHAN. Thank you, Mr. Hultgren. Thanks for being here.

We have gone through a lot. I have a—just one pointed question that I want to ask, and then if any other panelists has a specific follow-up question. You have talked a lot today about your work within the agency, so to speak, and the various components. We have heard from the Ranking Member about—how should I put it—competition within there that sometimes you have to ride over. So, you know, how do you discipline the organization to prevent these things?

You talk about sort-of the carrot approach, where you are trying to get people together and talk. But how do you assure that there is some kind of resolution of these competitions so we really use the focus to get to the things that matter the most? At the same time, how does the agency collaborate with the private sector? I think about the issue of cyber, where the thing changes by the day.

So research is being done at some of the most sophisticated places because you have got the Googles of the world, there and the Defense Department agencies, like McDonald Douglas or others that are already at the cutting edge protecting their—how do you collaborate with them to assure that your own house isn't fighting among itself? Then that what you are doing is working not in competition with the private sector, which may be ahead of where we are?

Under Secretary BROTHERS. I think cyber is a great example of the concern that you raise. I think we have done already—reached out to the Googles, et cetera of the world to try to understand, in this particular space, what we can do to try to bring together capabilities. I think it is important to reach out not just to small companies, as well. There is an awful lot of work going on in the small company space that we can leverage. But it is hard.

I mean, this is not an easy thing to do. But we are working right now, through our advisory, our Homeland Security Science and Advisory Committee, our HSSTAC. We are restructuring that to be both technical advisory as well as management strategic advisors. So we are putting—we are re-staffing that so that we can have the kinds of advisory——

Mr. MEEHAN. Do you have private-sector members on that, as well?

Under Secretary BROTHERS. We are working to get that, yes. Yes.

Mr. MEEHAN. You are looking at it, or you——

Under Secretary BROTHERS. We are looking at that. We are looking at that right now, yes. So that is how we are trying to get that advice. Because, particularly, cyber is such a fast-moving field, as you state, that it is important that we stay in touch with this ever-increasing body of work going on. There was a keynote speech at—one of the keynote speeches at the recent Black Hat Symposium, the cyber symposium, the speaker was talking about how it is almost impossible to be broad in cyber any longer. It is a—you know, now, in order to get ahead you have to be in a specific area because it is moving that fast. No one person can get their arms around the whole space. So that is why we have to reach out to our resources to do that.

The first question you asked, which had to do with, how do we influence? You mentioned——

Mr. MEEHAN. Well, you—I called it "discipline influence" that may be the same.

Under Secretary BROTHERS. I was trying to use the word "influence"?

[Laughter.]

Mr. MEEHAN. Yes, I like that terminology, so long as the result is the same.

Under Secretary BROTHERS. I think what I have learned from both working in industry, we have a large corporation that has different equities. So you have a large corporation where there are different products, product lines, but there might be common technologies that enable that. I think it is important that we stress why we are important. Because it is hard for—it is hard when you don't control someone else's budget, or people, to really discipline them. The discipline comes, I think, from saying—from being clear of why we are important. I think we are doing a better job of that already.

But I think we can do a better job of that. I think that is what we are gonna try to do. I know that is what we are gonna try to do.

Mr. MEEHAN. Well, I wish you luck with that effort because you know how critically important it is to make sure that the resources are focused in the most effective manner and not turf protection.

The gentleman now from New Jersey has some questions.

Mr. PAYNE. Thank you, Mr. Chairman. Let's see. Under Secretary Brothers, I am here at the behest of the Ranking Member, Yvette Clarke, but I am the Ranking Member on Emergency Preparedness, Response, and Communications. While I have you here, I figured I would go down that road a bit. The BioWatch program, we have been using Gen–2 for quite some time, and Gen–3 was in development but has been scuttled after millions and millions of dollars of research into the next generation.

Very interested in what your plans are in terms of the next steps, now that we are back to go and starting over. The relationship that you have with OHA which, apparently from what I am understanding, issues there—in the two coming together.

Under Secretary BROTHERS. I think—in the 4 months that I have been there, I think I get along pretty well with OHA, actually.

Mr. PAYNE. So the relationship, you think, is——

Under Secretary BROTHERS. I think it is. I think OHA would agree. In fact, I know they would, they have said this. So I think the relationship is a lot better. We are also—one of our Apex programs will be in this space. I am trying to go—we have a chance to go on for more signature-based, phenomenally-based, the same kind of thing that has been going in the cyber community. Kind-of taking lessons learned from other communities.

Mr. PAYNE. Right.

Under Secretary BROTHERS. But, yes. So we have not fully defined that yet, but we will—we are in the process of doing that.

Mr. PAYNE. I really think it is very important to move forward on that space, and finding a solution to the next generation of, you know, what could potentially be a catastrophic issue if——

Under Secretary BROTHERS. I absolutely agree with that.

Mr. PAYNE. Thank you, Mr. Chairman.

I yield back.

Under Secretary BROTHERS. Thank you.

Mr. MEEHAN. Any other Members have a question that they would like to ask, at this point? Okay.

Well, hearing none, I want to thank you—both of the panelists—not only for your testimony today, but for your preparation and written materials. Under Secretary, I thank you for your willingness to step into this space. You have an important challenge ahead, and we appreciate the difficulty of making the system work, the trains run on time, so to speak. But it is—the value of that effort reflects directly on the importance of the responsibility we have to protect the homeland. I wish you the best of luck in that.

Mr. Maurer, thank you for your continuing oversight and probing and finding the space, so to speak, for the mortar to fill.

So I want to thank you for your testimony, and the Members for their questions. The committee may have some additional questions for the witnesses, and we ask if they are submitted to you that you respond in writing.

Without objection, this subcommittee stands adjourned.

[Whereupon, at 11:44 a.m., the subcommittee was adjourned.]

APPENDIX

Question 1a. There has been quite a bit of discussion about Weapons of Mass Destruction (WMD) organizations across the U.S. Government, including DHS, DOD, and the IC (intelligence community). How would you define WMD? In other words, does it include chemical, biological, radiological, nuclear, and explosives? Would you also include cyber? Anything else?

Given that definition of WMD, from a scientific and technical perspective, what would you say is common to all the threats? Conversely, from a scientific and technical perspective, what would you say is different or unique?

Question 1b. In the Department, have you engaged in this type of discussion to develop better R&D and operational strategies to address these threats?

Answer. The Department of Homeland Security Lexicon defines WMD as "weapons capable of a high order of destruction and/or of being used in such a manner as to destroy large numbers of people or an amount of property." Even given this broad definition, there is a robust policy debate surrounding what should or should not be labeled as WMD. Traditionally, WMD describe chemical, biological, nuclear, and radiological weapons. All of these types of weapons have international treaties limiting their development and use, and much of the current debate focuses on potential disruption of these treaties should WMD be redefined to include explosives and/or cyber weapons. On the other side, there are arguments that WMD ought to be defined by their extreme level of disruption and that explosives and cyber weapons among others are justifiably considered WMD.

From a scientific and technical perspective, the differences for each of these threats (including cyber and explosives) include their specific origins and effects and corresponding requirements for threat-specialized technology and processes from initial detection through response and recovery. Regardless of whether cyber or explosives attacks are formally labeled as WMD, however, they are a priority for the Department and resourced accordingly both within the Directorate and DHS as a whole.

WMD and WMD-like events will all challenge the Homeland Security Enterprise's ability to generate and deliver actionable information so that senior decision makers and emergency managers can mitigate, to the extent possible, or neutralize destruction, disruption, and loss of life. At S&T and in the Department, we focus on both threat-specific technologies and on development of analytic tools, training aids, and decision-making aids that strengthen response across all WMD and WMD-like events. These types of threat-agnostic tools are reflected in S&T's recently-finalized visionary goals and in several of our Apex[1] and Engine projects. More broadly, the Department is concerned with all nefarious use of the causative agents and tends to use the label "CBRN" (chemical, biological, radiological, and nuclear) to capture them in a way that does not depend on the assumed scale of the attack.

As part of the Secretary's Unity of Effort initiative, the Department continues to explore avenues to empower DHS components to effectively execute their operations. S&T, the Office of Health Affairs, the Domestic Nuclear Detection Office, and the rest of the Department will continue to work together to develop better R&D and operational strategies to address chemical, biological, radiological, and nuclear threats.

Question 2a. According to authorities given to you in the Homeland Security Act of 2002, you have the responsibility for "establishing and administering the primary research and development activities for the Department."

---

[1] Apex projects are cross-cutting, multi-disciplinary efforts requested by DHS components that are high-priority, high-value, and short turn-around in nature. They are intended to solve problems of strategic operational importance identified by a component leader.

How is this being accomplished? Should other components (other than DNDO & Coast Guard which are already authorized in statute) be allowed to conduct their own R&D? How are you encouraging other components to work with S&T?

Answer. S&T is the primary provider of R&D for the Department. There are clear delineations between S&T, DNDO, and Coast Guard's missions, and DNDO and the Coast Guard also have clear authority to conduct R&D.

As part of original authorizing language and in response to subsequent Congressional requests, earlier this year, S&T finalized its plan for implementing the definition of R&D found in Office of Management and Budget Circular A–11. This mapping of the definition to DHS's project system variables also aligns with the Department of Defense designations tailored to DHS. It was signed by the Secretary as an annex to S&T's delegation. The definition describes several areas of later-stage development rightfully under the purview of operational components. These include, among others, validation and demonstration; improving on research prototypes; integration into systems and subsystems; addressing manufacturing, producibility, and sustainability needs; and independent operational test and evaluation. S&T cannot and should not take away responsibility for this stage of development from components. S&T provides assistance in these areas only when appropriate and when requested by operational partners.

S&T's impact is tied to positive relationships with operational components and S&T's image as an objective and trusted partner. S&T uses numerous formal and informal mechanisms to engage with components on R&D projects from identification of capability gaps, through project execution, all the way to transition. Some programs, like our Apexes, include formalized dialogue at the highest levels between S&T and our component partners. Other programs rely principally upon coordination at the program manager and Division leadership levels with approval from respective senior leaders. S&T has strong existing relationships with operators across the Homeland Security Enterprise, and we continuously work to maintain and strengthen these relationships and to find new opportunities and new potential work partners.

Question 2b. What specifically is DHS S&T doing to combat the cyber threat? Is S&T collaborating with NPPD to define a research agenda?

Answer. S&T invests in civilian and law enforcement-focused cybersecurity R&D solutions for the Department, U.S. critical infrastructure, and the security of the internet as a whole. S&T's cybersecurity R&D execution model encompasses the entire R&D life cycle from capability gaps gathering to program management of R&D work and, finally, to management of post-R&D technology transfer to ensure developed solutions have a positive impact on operations. S&T's work has improved the core infrastructure of the internet through efforts to secure the internet's Domain Name System and routing infrastructures. Since 2003, S&T has had more than 35 successful cybersecurity R&D transitions in areas such as malware analysis, anti-phishing technologies, data visualization, open-source intrusion prevention, secure USB devices, and GPS forensic analysis tools for law enforcement. Beyond the development of technologies, capabilities and standards, S&T's cybersecurity R&D work also contributes to the education and development of the cybersecurity workforce through activities such as sponsorship of cybersecurity competitions at the high school and collegiate levels (e.g., the National Collegiate Cyber Defense Competition).

S&T takes a collaborative approach to defining and executing its cybersecurity R&D agenda working with academia; DHS components (e.g., National Protection and Programs Directorate (NPPD), United States Secret Service (USSS), and U.S. Immigration and Customs Enforcement; Federal, State, and local government; private-sector partners (e.g., financial, energy); end-users; and numerous international partners. NPPD in particular was a key contributor to the development of requirements for a large-scale Broad Agency Announcement research solicitation that S&T issued in 2011, of which the majority of the resulting projects are completing in fiscal year 2015. The NPPD Office of Cybersecurity and Communications (CS&C) provided requirements for the solicitation's Software Assurance topic area, and the U.S. Computer Emergency Readiness Team provided requirements for the solicitation's Modeling of Internet Attacks, Network Mapping and Measurement, and Incident Response Communities topics. While developing a Cybersecurity R&D Strategy in 2013, S&T received input from multiple Government partners both from inside DHS (e.g., NPPD CS&C, USSS, Chief Information Security Officer) and outside (e.g., the White House, General Services Administration, Department of the Treasury, and Department of Energy) of DHS. Additional recent R&D requirements have come from the Comprehensive National Cybersecurity Initiative, the Federal Cybersecurity R&D Strategic Plan, and the DHS Blueprint for a Secure Cyber Future.

Question 2c. In times of declining budgets, how is S&T balancing the pressure to have short-term technology impact versus the need to invest in long-term technology solutions?

Answer. There is a natural and sometimes necessary temptation to resource incremental operational capabilities ahead of higher-risk, longer-term investments that are potentially much more innovative and beneficial. S&T recognizes the delicate balance between satisfying near-term requirements and keeping longer-term perspective and will continue to work with our operational partners to invest appropriately.

Following the steep decline in S&T's R&D appropriation from fiscal years 2010 to 2012, S&T was forced to make difficult decisions. Out of necessity, this included shifting the R&D portfolio toward less risky investments on shorter time lines that, as a tradeoff, were also potentially less innovative solutions. Moving forward, in response to feedback from our operational partners and homeland security stakeholders, S&T is pushing its R&D portfolio to be more aggressive with room for riskier investments that might yield revolutionary advances. To this end, S&T has made strategic decisions to generate visionary goals for the organization, expand Apex programs, and implement twice-per-year prioritization of its Research, Development, and Innovation (RD&I) portfolio.

S&T's long-term, visionary goals will serve as 30-year time line North Stars for the organization:

- *Screening at Speed.*—Security That Matches the Pace of Life
- *A Trusted Cyber Future.*—Protecting Privacy, Commerce, and Community
- *Enable the Decision Maker.*—Actionable Information at the Speed of Thought
- *Responder of the Future.*—Protected, Connected, and Fully Aware
- *Resilient Communities.*—Disaster-Proofing Society.

The goals strive for previously-unachieved capabilities or significantly lower-cost equivalents to existing capabilities. They will help orient our organization and inspire stakeholders, including operators, end-users, and performers in industry and academia, to focus on potential leap-ahead capabilities.

These visionary goals will be supported by Apex programs. S&T's existing Apex programs have been very successful. The core of the original Apex structure will remain—these will still be cross-cutting, multi-disciplinary efforts intended to solve problems of strategic operational importance—but, so that S&T's R&D portfolio is more balanced between near- and long-term outcomes, the programs will apply to a wider portion of the portfolio and operate on a 5-year time line, with interim deliverables planned in 2 to 3 years. To further amplify the effectiveness of these projects, S&T's priorities moving forward include better alignment of S&T resources like our Small Business Innovation Research awards and university-based Centers of Excellence and re-integration of basic scientific research that can be foundation for cutting-edge homeland security solutions.

Finally, prioritization of the R&D portfolio ensures funding of the highest-priority projects and gives an opportunity to balance the portfolio between long-term visions and short-term solutions. Continuous balancing ensures that S&T's investments will have the greatest impact in an era of declining budgets.

Question 2d. How does DHS strategically utilize and leverage expertise at the university and National laboratories?

Answer. Part of aligning all of S&T's resources moving forward will be ensuring we take advantage of the full spectrum of resources across what I refer to as the S&T Ecosystem, which is the broad network of technical expertise inside and outside of Government that can be brought to bear for virtually any issue operators face. Within this ecosystem, certain performers are particularly suited to certain needs. Universities and National Laboratories including S&T's internal laboratory network, with deep wells of expertise and investments in basic scientific research, are a critical part of the S&T Ecosystem.

The Department of Energy (DOE) National Laboratory Complex is the cornerstone of an integrated network of laboratory capabilities that support the S&T and DHS missions. The National labs provide multi-disciplinary, world-renowned capabilities that span all scientific and engineering disciplines. These capabilities provide solutions to S&T's and the DHS components' long-term technology challenges. In fiscal year 2013, DHS invested $262.7 million into the DOE labs to leverage these capabilities. The laboratories provide sustained research and development that support short- and long-term mission objectives. The Department's mission areas span a broad suite of scientific and technology disciplines, and National laboratories are adept at deploying well-integrated, interdisciplinary teams for their execution. Cooperation between S&T and DOE ranges from long-term capability planning such as at the Mission Executive Council to shorter-term tasking such as technology foraging to understand the current state of relevant technologies and laboratory capabilities. The labs' status as Federally-Funded Research and Development Centers permit the two parties to work outside the traditional competitive contractor framework for specialized strategic engagement.

In addition to DOE National laboratories, S&T manages five laboratories that provide strategic capabilities within the homeland security R&D portfolio including in biodefense, chemical security, transportation security, and first responders. These laboratories include the Chemical Security Analysis Center, providing chemical threat characterization and identification; the National Biodefense Analysis and Countermeasures Center, providing BSL–4 capability and forensic analysis and characterization; the National Urban Security Technology Laboratory, providing test and evaluation to first responder technologies; the Plum Island Animal Disease Center, providing animal disease characterization and identification; and the Transportation Security Laboratory, providing advancement in explosive and contraband detection. Each of these laboratories provides critical support to S&T, to other DHS components, and to the Homeland Security Enterprise.

Many of S&T's research contracts include or are based on work done with the Nation's best research universities. S&T also strategically uses the DHS University Centers of Excellence (COEs) and their partner networks in two ways. First, COEs conduct a wide range of R&D for S&T in support of DHS mission priorities that have been articulated through extensive partnerships with components. Second, through COEs, S&T provides DHS components and other Federal agencies with direct access to our universities' laboratories, expertise, and analytical capabilities to conduct their own short- and long-term R&D. Their use of the Centers is facilitated through streamlined contract and financial assistance mechanisms in ten targeted research areas. The COEs' successful research results, as well as S&T processes that allow easy access to COEs, have attracted more than $96 million in additional funding from DHS components and offices and other Federal agencies since 2007. Each COE works with S&T, other Federal agencies, and end-users to address user-identified challenges including resilience, law enforcement, hurricanes, biodefense, risk assessment, terrorism, and data analytics. More than 150 individual customers in offices across DHS have relied on the Centers to address complex and persistent challenges, deliver technical solutions, and build a highly specialized workforce.

Question 2e. How can S&T ensure that it is aware of all of the R&D activities occurring within the Department?

Answer. The establishment of an R&D definition was an important first step. Moving forward, S&T will draft a directive and instruction for formal coordination of R&D in the Department. This is still a work in progress, but potential ideas include an annually updated overview of R&D within the Department, cross-Department R&D strategic information sharing similar to the Department of Defense, and formal establishment of a two-way embed program between S&T and operational elements. As this plan crystallizes further within DHS, we look forward to sharing it with you and your fellow committee Members and staff.

Question 3a. According to CRS the Homeland Security Advanced Research Projects Agency (HSARPA) with in S&T was originally developed to be modeled after the DOD R&D agency DARPA.

Is this the proper model for HSPARA and should the two even be compared given the dramatic differences in the scope, scale, and budget of each organization?

Question 3b. How should HSARPA be designed and set up to fit the needs and scale of DHS?

Answer. No, DARPA would not be an appropriate model for DHS's R&D organization. Despite original authorizing language modeling HSARPA as a DARPA-like R&D provider for DHS, several meaningful differences between HSARPA and DARPA have emerged as the Department and S&T have matured. In fiscal year 2014, DARPA was appropriated nearly $3 billion compared to approximately $417 million for HSARPA. Unlike DARPA, HSARPA is not backed by an industrial base equivalently resourced and capable to the Defense Industrial Base. HSARPA also serves customer bases that, unlike warfighters, operate at a much lower cost point and typically do not have as much time available to train and integrate new technology into their operations.

Perhaps most significantly, the role that S&T and HSARPA have grown into within the Department is much less specialized than DARPA's role within DOD. At DOD, R&D is a multi-faceted construct with different organizations specialized to different stages of the process to nurture technology to operational use. DARPA was originally chartered to "prevent technological surprise". As a result, while DARPA focuses nearly exclusively on providing basic through applied research, S&T and HSARPA are responsible for the full life cycle of technology development and transition for not only the DHS operational components but also the Homeland Security Enterprise as a whole. With about a tenth of DARPA's discretionary budget (DARPA does not manage labs or Centers of Excellence), S&T has a much broader mission. Additional roles filled by S&T include understanding the mission and operational need (in DOD, the role of a branch-specific organization like the Office of Naval Research) and development of business requirements, operational application, and transition (in DOD, the role of a branch's-specific organization like the Naval Sea Systems Command).

HSARPA does not require drastic changes or new authorities to fulfill its mission. The Under Secretary for Science and Technology has sufficient latitude and authority to shape HSARPA to meet the needs of both the Department and the wider Homeland Security Enterprise. We recognize the critical differences between DARPA, HSARPA, and their roles in their respective Departments and have adjusted how we conduct ourselves accordingly.

For example, to meet the needs of our customers, our R&D portfolio is generally much more geared toward near- and medium-term operational application than DARPA. In addition, since operational partners also rely on S&T for potential leap-ahead technology, we also ensure that our portfolio still invests in projects with higher risk but correspondingly higher reward. Examples will include S&T's expanded Apex projects, which will be high-value, 5-year horizon projects focused on a DHS component's unique mission and capability needs. Recently-finalized visionary goals will help orient S&T and inspire stakeholders, including operators, end-users, and performers in industry and academia, toward the types of revolutionary capabilities that the Directorate will focus on. In order to work meaningfully toward these types of 30-year-horizon North Stars, we are also expanding our Apex programs and focusing on alignment of all of S&T's capabilities in support of those programs. Taken altogether, these are examples of how S&T and HSARPA, despite being different from DARPA, are aligned to meet the needs of the Department and the Homeland Security Enterprise.

Question 4. Given GAO's concerns that DHS does not know how much it invests in R&D, can S&T produce a reliable list of R&D projects and associated costs occurring throughout the Department? If so, please include that list in this response. If not, why not?

Answer. In fiscal year 2014, the Department's budget included approximately $1.032 billion for R&D including $932 million at S&T (including $433 million related to laboratory infrastructure investments such as construction of the National Bio and Agro-Defense Facility) and approximately $100 million more at Coast Guard's Research and Development Center and in the Domestic Nuclear Detection Office research budget. In addition, S&T's Research, Development, Acquisition, and Operations budget included $115 million for laboratory operations, $42 million for acquisition and operations analysis, and $3 million for Minority Serving Institutions.

Under the DHS-specific definition of R&D signed by the Secretary as an annex to S&T's delegation, there are several additional areas of later-stage development rightfully under the purview of operational components including, among others, validation and demonstration; improving on research prototypes; integration into systems and subsystems; addressing manufacturing, producibility, and sustainability needs; and independent operational test and evaluation.

The next step will be using this definition to develop a more complete picture of the Department's R&D that includes on-going late-stage development efforts by components. In fiscal year 2015, S&T is helping write a Directive and Instruction, developed in partnership with components, for more information sharing and tighter collaboration between S&T and operational elements of DHS. S&T looks forward to sharing this information with Congress when results have been finalized.

Question 5. Does DHS S&T utilize relevant research from the National Science Foundation, for instance research conducted related to cybersecurity or behavioral research? If so, can you provide me with a list of specific examples of NSF-sponsored work DHS S&T has utilized?

Answer. Yes, S&T works with the National Science Foundation (NSF) in behavioral, biological, and cybersecurity research areas. In August 2010, the S&T Actionable Indicators and Countermeasures project entered an interagency agreement with NSF to conduct research focused on the U.S. public's attitudes toward terrorism and counterterrorism activities. S&T provided NSF with funding to support several surveys on this topic as part of the Time-Sharing Experiments for Social Sciences project, leveraging an existing NSF-sponsored research infrastructure to produce findings in the most cost-effective manner possible.

S&T is an affiliate in the NSF Center for Identity Technology Research (CITeR), a NSF Industry/University Cooperative Research Center (I/UCRC) that DHS has contributed to for the last 11 years. More than 250 university research projects have been jointly conducted through CITeR jointly, including these examples:

- Cross-Device and Cross-Distance Matching Face Recognition Using Cell Phones with Enhanced Camera Capabilities (University at Buffalo)
- Fingerprint Identification: A Longitudinal Study (Michigan State University)
- Fusing Biometric and Biographic Information in Identification Systems (Michigan State and West Virginia Universities)
- Touch DNA: Fusing Latent Fingerprint with DNA for Suspect Identification (West Virginia University)

S&T's Cyber Security Division has several active efforts with NSF. First, the Transition to Practice (TTP) program identifies mature cybersecurity technologies developed with Government funding and then funds test and evaluation and operational pilots for these technologies to speed their path to operational use and/or commercialization. Through TTP technology foraging with NSF, two NSF-funded cybersecurity technologies, AMICO and ZeroPoint, have been brought into the portfolio for potential pilot and transition to wider operational use. Second, S&T and NSF will jointly fund three Cyber Physical Systems-related research efforts with NSF—two focusing on the smart grid and a third focusing on smart manufacturing. Finally, S&T funds software assurance research projects through the Security and Software Engineering Research Center (S2ERC), another NSF I/UCRC with projects including a software quality assurance tool study to help identify gaps in current software quality assurance tools and a technology to identify architecturally significant code in systems and applications that could lead to potential vulnerabilities.

In fiscal year 2007, DHS and NSF initiated joint funding for the National Institute for Mathematical and Biological Synthesis (NIMBioS), to promote the development of cross-disciplinary approaches and new collaborations in mathematical biology, including infectious disease dynamics. While the focus of NIMBioS is much broader than foreign animal disease threats, or even infectious disease dynamics, many of the new innovations that arise as a result of the Institute's activities will be widely applicable in these areas. The Institute sponsors a range of activities at the interface of mathematics and biology, including research and education, collaborations with other relevant scientific disciplines (e.g., computer science, ecology), human resource development (e.g., science fairs for children and parents), and questions concerned with public policy (e.g., animal depopulation as a strategy for control of animal diseases). Furthermore, NIMBioS engages a range of participants. While the majority are academics (college or university faculty or staff, graduate students, or undergraduates), a number of participants are from Government, private sector, or non-profits. DHS's last year of funding for NIMBioS was fiscal year 2012 (to refocus on more tool-oriented modeling approaches), but NSF independently renewed the Institute's funding for another 5-year term. S&T continues to participate in reviews of the programs, and our programs continue to benefit from the results of these investments.

QUESTIONS FROM CHAIRMAN LAMAR S. SMITH FOR REGINALD BROTHERS

Question 1. Who are the entities/stakeholders responsible for securing the border? How do they determine whether solutions require technology, people, training, and/or policy and procedures?

Question 2. What activities is the S&T Directorate currently undertaking to improve border security?

Answer. Securing the land, maritime, and air borders is a collaborative effort among S&T, DNDO, and the operating components of DHS, including the United States Customs and Border Protection (CBP), U.S. Immigration and Customs Enforcement, Transportation Security Administration (TSA), and the United States Coast Guard (USCG). S&T is the primary research and development arm for DHS and manages research, from development through transition, for the Department's operational components, with DNDO having the equivalent responsibility for nuclear and radiological detection and forensics. S&T works with the DHS operational components to identify capability gaps and to determine if people, training, readily available commercial technologies, policy/procedures, or new technology is needed to fulfill the requirement. S&T will typically perform market research or technology foraging to discover, adapt, and/or leverage technology solutions developed by other Governmental and private-sector entities to address the gap. If there are no existing solutions, S&T will seek to develop a new solution through Federal and private partnerships and collaborations, or on its own to fulfill the gap.

S&T's Borders and Maritime Security Division, in its pursuit of technology to enhance border security, categorizes its efforts as follows: (1) Land Border Security (between the Ports of Entry (POEs)), (2) Maritime Border Security, and (3) Cargo Security (at the POEs). The activities being undertaken in each category are discussed below.

LAND BORDER SECURITY (BETWEEN THE POES)

In support of CBP's Offices of Border Patrol and Air and Marine (OAM), S&T is pursuing technology solutions in the following areas:

Improved Utilization of Air Platform-Based Technologies.—Identifying, testing, and evaluating air-based technologies to improve CBP's ability to detect, classify, and track illicit activity. The use of sensors on fixed and rotary wing, manned and unmanned aircraft will provide improved situational awareness that will in turn improve decision making at both the local and regional level.

Improved Ground-Based Technologies.—Developing technology to fill capability gaps on both Northern and Southern Borders identified by the Border Surveillance Working Group (made up of Border Patrol personnel and other subject-matter experts). This includes work developing and piloting border tripwires, unattended ground sensors, camera poles, upgrades to mobile surveillance units, etc. These efforts will allow for improved situational awareness of the U.S. terrestrial borders resulting in higher interdiction rates and better utilization of Border Patrol Agents and assets.

Rapid Prototyping.—Rapidly assessing and deploying commercial-off-the-shelf (COTS) or near-COTS solutions in response to critical border security needs identified by CBP. The project will result in rapid adoption of technology, improving CBP's capabilities and/or reduce operations and maintenance costs.

Improved Tunnel Detection and Tunnel Forensics.—Developing technologies to detect and locate clandestine tunnels used to smuggle drugs and contraband into the United States along the Southern Border. This also includes developing tools to obtain forensic evidence from discovered tunnels to support investigations and increase arrests and prosecutions. Efforts will result in an increase in the number of tunnels detected and will reduce the flow of contraband smuggled into the United States.

Improved Border Situational Awareness (Apex Project).—Improving border situational awareness along the Southwestern U.S. Border by: (1) Integrating existing sensor and non-sensor data, (2) providing decision support tools that will translate data into actionable information, and (3) enabling data and information sharing across the Homeland Security Enterprise (Federal, State, local, Tribal, and international). This integrated border information enterprise will enable effective law enforcement response at the local level while allowing risk-based resource allocation at the local, sector, and National level. This will result in more effective and efficient border security, improving interdiction rates, keeping more drugs off of U.S. streets while reducing human trafficking and illegal immigration.

MARITIME BORDER SECURITY

In support of CBP's OAM and USCG, S&T is pursuing technology solutions in the following areas:

Improved Arctic Communications Capability.—Identifying and evaluating candidate terrestrial and space-based solutions to inform the acquisition and implementation of reliable communications in the Arctic. Reliable communications are essential for safe and effective operations as the Coast Guard extends its mission into the Arctic.

Enhanced Port and Coastal Surveillance.—Developing solutions to improve maritime situational awareness, information/data analytics, and information sharing, which will enable appropriate and effective response to maritime threats. Technical solutions will: (1) Enable rapid tactical response resulting in increased interdiction efficiency, (2) enable risk-based strategic planning/resource allocation, and (3) enhance officer effectiveness, efficiency, and safety.

CARGO SECURITY (AT THE POES)

In support of CBP's Office of Field Operations (OFO), S&T is pursuing technology solutions in the following areas:

Improved Cargo Container Security.—Developing technologies for collecting additional cargo security data, while also investing in analysis methods for transforming new and existing cargo security data into actionable information in the form of improved targeting that will lead to a higher probability of detecting illegal or hazardous materials in cargo while expediting the delivery of legitimate cargo. The impact will be a reduction of the number of containers requiring scanning and/or manual inspection saving CBP millions annually in labor and facility costs while increasing the throughput of legitimate cargo.

Enhanced Cargo Validation Capability.—Providing CBP with the capability to detect the transport of contraband, counterfeit merchandise, or invasive species in inbound and out-bound cargo at the POEs and detect and prosecute illegal activity through the forensic analysis of material collected from suspicious cargo/packages. The result will be an increase in throughput of legitimate cargo, an increase in the availability of forensic evidence enabling enhanced trade compliance enforcement, and a reduction in the cost to industry caused by delays at the POE.

Improved Cargo Scanning Capability.—Developing software and hardware upgrades for legacy cargo scanning units and infusing state-of-the-art technology to enhance their detection performance and extend their service life. S&T is also developing/prototyping tools to non-intrusively scan structural voids for hidden contraband in automobiles and other cargo conveyances. The technology will enhance CBP's effectiveness in detecting contraband at POEs while increasing the throughput of legitimate cargo. S&T is also working with the Domestic Nuclear Detection Office to develop and test new technology that fuses nuclear detection with the detection of other contraband.

Should Members of the committee be interested in further information about any of the above programs, S&T would be happy to provide more detailed briefings.

QUESTION FROM RANKING MEMBER DANIEL LIPINSKI FOR REGINALD BROTHERS

Question. In your opening statement you said, "With S&T's reauthorization, the committee has an opportunity to help launch a 21st Century research and development (R&D) organization that will serve as a model for Federal R&D." In the context of reauthorizing S&T, what would be your legislative recommendations to the committees that would put you in a better position to launch a 21st Century R&D organization? What are the top five high-priority items you would you like to see in the reauthorization?

Answer. Empowering an R&D organization for the 21st Century means providing organizational flexibility to empower a technical workforce capable of more open and effective engagement with the full breadth of industry and other non-Government stakeholders. Many of the mechanisms and constraints that S&T and other Federal R&D organizations operate under are the result of authorities suited to a different era with less competition for technical expertise and less emphasis on organizational agility and responsiveness to rapid change.

The homeland security mission space encompasses numerous complex threats that evolve quickly and consistently strain operational resources. Our partners rely on S&T to identify and exploit technology-based opportunities to jump the threat curve and gain an advantage. S&T, as the R&D organization supporting these operators, would achieve its mission more effectively if it were given greater flexibility and empowerment in re-authorization. Examples of revised or new authorities include permanent Other Transaction Authority for S&T, which would allow more strategic use by avoiding prolonged lapses in the authority, and moving AD 1101 hiring authority out of the Homeland Security Advanced Research Projects Agency to the Under Secretary for Science and Technology level, which would grant hiring flexibility to meet technical needs throughout the directorate.

Moving forward, endorsement by the committee of S&T's approach would also help us maintain and expand upon progress made to date. That includes our planned implementation of a robust process for S&T's workforce to embed with operators and to allow operational staff to detail to S&T and provide direct input to our R&D projects. That also includes our modified approach to the R&D portfolio, which includes expansion of our Apexes and establishment of cross-cutting Engines that support R&D work throughout S&T.

QUESTIONS FROM HONORABLE CHRIS COLLINS FOR REGINALD BROTHERS

Question 1. What different types of technologies are being pursued by DHS for detection of infectious diseases?

Question 2. How is DHS ensuring the technologies they are developing do not overlap with those of DoD when it comes to infectious diseases (i.e. anthrax and other airborne toxins)?

Answer. S&T has several projects focused on improvements for detection and identification of infectious diseases. These range from laboratory assays to fieldable devices to data analytics for rapid situational awareness.

S&T is working collaboratively with an interagency group that includes DoD to develop, test, evaluate, and validate highly specific and sensitive laboratory assays for the rapid detection of disease agents. These assays are intended for both clinical diagnostic use as well as environmental sample analysis, and will be deployed and employed through the more than 150 CDC Laboratory Response Network laboratories across the Nation for comprehensive coverage and rapid response to a biological incident.

During a biological event, one potential problem will be pathogens with resistance or immunity to existing medical countermeasures. Overuse and inappropriate use of medical countermeasures in the United States and internationally (i.e., use of antibacterial countermeasures for viral infections) have resulted in many bacterial pathogens with resistances that threaten the efficacy and utility of antibiotics. As a result, the White House recently initiated a program called "Combating Antimicrobial Resistant Bacteria." S&T is supporting technology that will rapidly determine whether infections are bacterial versus viral and help medical professionals decide when antibiotics should be prescribed. This will ultimately lead to prudent use of life-saving medical countermeasures that will prolong their life span and utility to the Nation and medical community in the case of a biological event.

Effective response to emerging infectious disease will also require information sharing between local hospitals, State public health departments, and Federal agencies. S&T is undertaking efforts to evaluate information communication systems and data analytic techniques that will facilitate rapid awareness of a disease emergence for effective public safety communication and response.

In all of these programs, S&T engages key Federal partners, including multiple organizations within DoD, to participate in capability gap generation processes and program execution to ensure that there is no duplication of effort. There are jointly funded DHS-DoD projects, technical exchanges around biosurveillance and biodetection activities, and a Memorandum of Understanding that establishes a formal information-sharing mechanisms between S&T and DoD Office of the Secretary of Defense.

QUESTION FROM CHAIRMAN LAMAR S. SMITH FOR DAVID C. MAURER

Question. Who are the entities/stakeholders responsible for securing the border? How do they determine whether solutions require technology, people, training, and/or policy and procedures?

Answer. Securing U.S. borders is the responsibility of the Department of Homeland Security (DHS), in collaboration with other Federal, State, local, and Tribal entities. U.S. Customs and Border Protection (CBP), a component within DHS that is the lead agency for border security, is responsible, among other things, for preventing terrorists and their weapons of terrorism from entering the United States and for interdicting persons and contraband crossing the border illegally. Within CBP, the Office of Field Operations (OFO) is responsible for securing the border at ports of entry (POE)[1] and the U.S. Border Patrol (Border Patrol) is the CBP component charged with ensuring security along border areas between the POEs. Additionally, CBP's Office of Air and Marine (OAM) provides air and maritime support to secure the National border between the POEs, within maritime operating areas, and within the Nation's interior. The U.S. Coast Guard executes its maritime security mission on and over the major waterways, including the Great Lakes, using marine and air assets.

DHS and CBP and its components coordinate their border security efforts with various Federal, State, local, Tribal, and foreign law enforcement agencies that also have responsibilities to detect, interdict, and investigate different types of illegal activity within certain geographic boundaries. For example, U.S. Department of Agriculture (USDA) and Department of Interior (DOI) agencies have jurisdiction for law enforcement on Federal borderlands including nearly 2,000 miles of Federally-owned or -managed land adjacent to the international borders with Canada and Mexico administered by their component agencies. These component agencies—including DOI's National Park Service, Fish and Wildlife Service, and Bureau of Land Management and USDA's Forest Service—are responsible for the protection of natural and cultural resources, agency personnel, and the public on the lands they administer. In addition, DOI's Bureau of Indian Affairs may enforce Federal laws on Indian lands with the consent of Tribes and in accordance with Tribal laws, and law enforcement personnel from sovereign Indian nations located on the international borders also conduct law enforcement operations related to border security. International partners in securing the U.S. border include Canadian and Mexican law enforcement agencies.

In addition, there are other Federal, State, and local partners in securing the U.S. border. These partners include DHS's U.S. Immigration and Customs Enforcement (ICE) which is responsible for investigating the source of cross-border crimes and dismantling illegal operations. Partners at the Department of Justice (DOJ) include the Drug Enforcement Administration (DEA), which conducts investigations of pri-

---

[1] Ports of entry are officially designated places that provide for the arrival at or departure from the United States.

ority drug-trafficking organizations, domestic and foreign, that can include drug smuggling across the border or ports of entry and the Federal Bureau of Investigation (FBI), which has responsibility for combating terrorism. The Department of Defense (DOD), while not a partner, also provides support as requested, such as personnel and technology for temporary joint operations. Moreover, numerous State and local law enforcement entities interdict and investigate criminal activity on public and private lands adjacent to the border. Although these agencies are not responsible for preventing the illegal entry of aliens into the United States, they do employ law enforcement officers and investigators to protect the public and natural resources on their lands.

We have reported on CBP's processes for identifying border security resource needs, specifically related to Border Patrol resources for securing the Southwest Border between ports of entry, deployments of air and marine resources by CBP's OAM, and technology deployment along the Southwest Border. With regard to Border Patrol resource needs, in December 2012 we reported on the extent to which Border Patrol developed mechanisms to identify resources needed to secure the border under its new strategic plan, issued in May 2012.[2] We reported that as the Border Patrol began transitioning to its new strategic plan, it has been using an interim process for assessing the need for additional personnel, infrastructure, and technology in agency sectors. Border Patrol officials told us that under the risk management approach called for in the Border Patrol's fiscal year 2012–2016 strategic plan, the need for additional resources would be determined in terms of unacceptable levels of risk caused by illegal activity across border locations. Until a new process for identifying resource needs has been developed, we reported that Border Patrol sectors would continue to use annual operational assessments to reflect specific objectives and measures for accomplishing annual sector priorities, as well as identifying minimum budgetary requirements necessary to maintain the current status of border security in each sector. We recommended, among other things, that CBP establish milestones and time frames for developing performance measures for assessing progress made in securing the border and for informing resource identification and allocation efforts. DHS concurred with our recommendation and is working to establish such milestones and time frames.

In addition to assessing Border Patrol's processes for identifying resource needs, we have reported on identification and allocation of resources for CBP's Office of Air and Marine. The Office of Air and Marine provides aircraft, vessels, and crew at the request of its customers, primarily Border Patrol. In March 2012, we reported that the Office of Air and Marine had not documented significant events, such as its analyses to support its asset mix and placement across locations, and as a result, lacked a record to help demonstrate that its decisions to allocate resources were the most effective ones in fulfilling customer needs and addressing threats.[3] The Office of Air and Marine issued various plans that included strategic goals, mission responsibilities, and threat information. However, we were unable to identify the underlying analyses used to link these factors to the mix and placement of resources across locations because the Office of Air and Marine did not have documentation that clearly linked the deployment decisions in the plan to mission needs or threats. Similarly, we found that the Office did not document analyses supporting the current mix and placement of marine assets across locations. Office of Air and Marine headquarters officials stated that they made deployment decisions during formal discussions and on-going meetings in close collaboration with Border Patrol, and considered a range of factors such as operational capability, mission priorities, and threats. Officials said that while they generally documented final decisions affecting the mix and placement of resources, they did not have the resources to document assessments and analyses to support these decisions. However, we reported that such documentation of significant events could help the Office improve the transparency of its resource allocation decisions to help demonstrate the effectiveness of these resource decisions in fulfilling its mission needs and addressing threats. We recommended that CBP document analyses, including mission requirements and threats that support decisions on the mix and placement of the Office's air and marine resources. DHS concurred with our recommendation and stated that it plans to provide additional documentation of its analyses supporting decisions on the mix and placement of air and marine resources.

CBP also has a planning process for acquiring and deploying surveillance technologies along the Southwest Border. For example, In November 2011, we reported

---

[2] GAO, *Border Patrol: Key Elements of New Strategic Plan Not Yet in Place to Inform Border Security Status and Resource Needs,* GAO–13–25 (Washington, DC: Dec. 10, 2012).

[3] GAO, *Border Security: Opportunities Exist to Ensure More Effective Use of DHS's Air and Marine Assets,* GAO–12–518 (Washington, DC: Mar. 30, 2012).

on CBP's plan to identify, acquire, and deploy surveillance technologies along the Arizona border.[4] This plan, referred to as the Arizona Border Surveillance Technology Plan, is the first step in DHS's approach for acquiring and deploying border security technologies, such as surveillance systems, hand-held equipment, and unattended ground sensors, along the Southwest Border.

We reported that CBP used a two-step process to develop the Arizona Border Surveillance Technology Plan. First, CBP engaged the Homeland Security Studies and Analysis Institute to conduct an analysis of alternatives beginning with Arizona.[5] This analysis of alternatives considered four technology alternatives: (1) Agent-centric hand-held devices, (2) integrated fixed-tower systems, (3) mobile surveillance equipment, and (4) unmanned aerial vehicles. In its analysis of alternatives, the Homeland Security Studies and Analysis Institute noted that its analysis did not, among other things, identify the optimal combination of specific equipment and systems, measure the contribution of situational awareness to achieving control of the border, or quantify the number of apprehensions that may result from the deployment of any technology solution. According to officials from the Homeland Security Studies and Analysis Institute, the Institute assembled an independent review team composed of senior subject-matter experts with expertise in border security, operational testing, acquisition, performance measurement, and the management and execution of analyses of alternatives to evaluate the analysis of alternatives for Arizona. In the results of the final report, the review team from the Homeland Security Studies and Analysis Institute concluded that the analysis of alternatives for Arizona appeared to have successfully answered the questions asked and drew appropriate conclusions and insights that should be useful to DHS and CBP.

Second, we reported that following the completion of the analysis of alternatives, the Border Patrol conducted its operational assessment, which included a comparison of alternative border surveillance technologies and an analysis of operational judgments to consider both effectiveness and cost. According to CBP officials, they started with the results of the analysis of alternatives for Arizona, noting that the analysis considered the technologies in terms of the trade-offs between capability and cost—but did not document the quantities of each technology needed, the appropriate mix of the technologies, or how a proposed mix of technologies would be applied to specific border areas. CBP officials stated that a team of Border Patrol Agents familiar with the Arizona terrain determined the appropriate quantity and mix of technologies by considering the terrain in each area under consideration and which mix of technologies appeared to work for that area and terrain.

We found that while the first step in CBP's process to develop the Arizona Border Surveillance Technology Plan—the analysis of alternatives—was well documented, the second step—Border Patrol's operational assessment—was not transparent because of the lack of documentation. Specifically, CBP did not document its analysis justifying the specific types, quantities, and deployment locations of border surveillance technologies CBP proposed in its plan. We recommended that CBP ensure that the underlying analyses of the plan are documented. While DHS concurred with our recommendation, officials noted that CBP was not planning further analyses or additional documentation given that they consider their analyses to be sufficiently documented in the final plan. Given that CBP has moved forward in awarding contracts for the Plan's technology programs and does not plan to conduct further analyses, we closed this recommendation as not implemented. In addition, DHS noted that it relies on Border Patrol field agents' expert judgment to select the type and quantities of technologies best suited for their respective geographic areas of responsibilities, and that technology selections were verified for consistency with the major findings of the analysis of alternatives.

○

---

[4] GAO, *Arizona Border Surveillance Technology: More Information on Plans and Costs Is Needed before Proceeding*, GAO–12–22 (Washington, DC: Nov. 4, 2011).

[5] The Homeland Security Studies and Analysis Institute is a Federally-funded research and development center to provide independent analysis of homeland security issues.

www.ingramcontent.com/pod-product-compliance
Lightning Source LLC
Chambersburg PA
CBHW080535290526
45790CB00006B/2422